Integrity:

An Act Of Distinction

Integrity:

An Act Of Distinction

Emmanuel Goshen

Published by Edson Consultancy

© Copyright Edson Consultancy 2017

INTEGRITY:
AN ACT OF DISTINCTION

All rights reserved.

The right of Emmanuel Goshen to be identified as the author of this work has been asserted in accordance with the Copyright, Designs and Patents Act 1988.

No part of this publication may be reproduced, stored in a retrieval sytem, or transmitted, in any form or by any means, electronic, mechanical, photocopying, recording or otherwise, nor translated into a machine language, without the written permission of the publisher.

Condition of sale

This book is sold subject to the condition that it shall not, by way of trade or otherwise, be lent, re-sold, hired out or otherwise circulated in any form of binding or cover other than that in which it is published and without a similar condition including this condition being imposed on the subsequent purchaser.

ISBN 978-0-995-74680-0

Printed and bound in the United Kingdom

CONTENTS

DEDICATION i
ACKNOWLEDGEMENT ii
PREFACE v
INTRODUCTION 1
WHY INTEGRITY? 10
THE ACT OF ACCOUNTABILITY 23
THE ACT OF ACCESSIBILITY 33
THE ACT OF COMPETENCY 44
THE ACT OF CONTENTMENT 51
THE ACT OF EQUALITY 74
THE ACT OF LOYALTY 81
THE ACT OF RELIABILITY 86
THE ACT OF TRANSPARENCY 97
THE ACT OF DISTINCTION 104
TAKE THIS HOME 118

OTHER BOOKS BY EMMANUEL GOSHEN

1. The leader's supplement: A major platform for high performance leadership
2. The 7 Laws of Productivity: Make Your Vision a Reality
3. The 7 Principles of Transformation: Accomplishing your goals with the right insight
4. The Mysteries of Excellence: Graduating from Challenges to a Champion Arena

To my lovely sons, Edward and Edwin

DEDICATION

The success of this book is dedicated to the Almighty God, the foundation and pillar of wisdom. The One who inspired me to write this book.

ACKNOWLEDGEMENT

I will sing of the mercies of the Lord for ever: with my mouth will I make known thy faithfulness to all generations. (Psalm 89:1) (KJV). I would forever remain grateful to the only who makes the impossibilities possible, unto whom thousands of tongues shall remain and would remain insufficient to praise him name, to the greatest one who rolled back the waters of the might Red Sea, I remain appreciative to him. To the only one who brought me this far in mist of challenges by grace, I bless his holy name.

    I would like to appreciate my family members and friends for their various supports over the years. I wouldn't walk pass the other side without appreciating my wife Rachel for her huge sacrifice regarding my career as an author. To my mother, Pastor Mrs. Victoria Majekodunmi, and father, Engineer James Majekodunmi I say thank you for your inspirational words in bringing me up. I appreciate Prophet Adefenwa and his family and Mr and Mrs Ajibade. My thanks also go to my uncle Mr. Solomon Majekodunmi, and Prophet Moses Olurin and his family for their support and prayers. To my friend who acted and stood as a twin brother at the point reality, who sheltered during the shameful and unexpected rain, the real son of the soil, Mr Emmanuel Olusegun Akinola, yourself and your wonderful family shall always be remembered in prayers and thoughts. To Prophet Larry Frank, Apostle Sheriff Jacobs, Pastor Agbaeze Okorie Ugorji , Mr and Mrs Adelegan, Evangelist (Dr) Raymond Tade Tayo, Evangelist Adeniyi Adenuga, Pastor Yomi Peters and Rev Joseph Fasogbon, Archbishop David Fabusoro I appreciate you all for your immeasurable love and support.

To my wonderful friends Mr John Threlfall, Mrs Irene Agunbiade, Mr Badru Temitope, Dr John Lang, Mr and Mrs Olagbaju, Prophet John Martins, Mr and Mrs Monume, Evangelist Wale Onafuye, Evangelist Yomi King, Evangelist Emmanuel Ogunlade, Merrie Joy Williams, Mr Christian Okpara, Mr and Mrs West, Prophet George Olamide Akinsulire, Mr and Mrs Adenubi, Mr and Mrs Edwin Mante, Mr and Mrs Samson Tawio, Mr and Mrs Ologbonori, Prince Lasun Adele and his family. You are all wonderful and I love you all, it's my prayer that higher may the grace of the almighty God be upon us all.

To a lovely father in Christ, Evangelist Moses Kolawole Solaru who stood beside me and instilled the required wisdom to help me through rough times and become the man I am today, the unbeatable fact of history would foster reality and you can never be forgotten in my mind. Never would I walk pass through this side without appreciating another father, brother and friend Evangelist Paul Babatunde Soile and his wonderful family for their passionate love and support in which mere words can't describe. My thanks likewise go to Dr. David Soile, Dr Tayo Ogunmefun, Madam Elizabeth Abimbola James and Evangelist Richard Dele Moronfolu for their outstanding love and words of encouragement. I cannot forget to be grateful to my class teacher and Brother Mr Sunday Banjo and his family. I would like to appreciate Evangelist Abraham O Ayoade for his professional advice.

The following people at one time or the other have touched my life and I must be very thankful to them; they include Dr. Oluwasegun King and his family whose inspired me to write this book, Dr. Deborah Titilayo Nunayon, Mr. and Mrs. A. A. Ademola, Prophet Elijah Alabede, , Madam Sheri Adekomolafe Edu, Dr. Martin Ehigianusoe will always be remembered in my prayers for the amount of time and effort he invested in making this book a reality. I feel humbled and respectful in appreciating Venerable Superior Evangelist Olusegun Olarinde, Venerable Superior Evangelist Amos Fatusin, Mr and Mrs Apanisile, Mr. and Mrs. Alayo, and Madam Fatima Tiamiyu Abioye, Pastor Yinka Ogunlola and his family, Pastor Samuel Donkor, John Adeyinka, , Ms. Busayo Asade, Maria Olubunmi, for your love and contributions in making this book a reality. Mrs. Philippa Gittens and her lovely family are worth to me more than any kind of treasures and have a special place in my little heart for their encouragement, which enabled me to go miles further than I thought possible. I would like to appreciate the wonderful effort of my editor Cynthia Calzone and proof reader Nikola (Nick) Sablic.

PREFACE

Having read a book on strategic implementation some years ago, I was impressed by the story of a rich man who had the intention of opening a large fast-food company in a certain community. The rich man was able to buy out the lease of three shops in a chain of four shops, but the remaining shop was located in the middle of the four shops. The fact was, there was no way he could operate a decent business because he needed to link the four shops and reconstruct them to his taste. However, the current manager of the middle shop, which happened to be a traditional fish and chips shop and also a family-run business since the early eighteenth century, had refused to lease the shop to the rich man, regardless of the huge offers being made. The fish and chips business was well known for its uniqueness, quality, and service which set it above the other local competitors. After building the reputation of the business over the years, the owning family treasured the business, which was valued at over ten times the average market value price.

Having waited for a long time, putting his plans on hold and finding the manager to be a major obstacle in his path, the rich man decided to pay his best friend a huge sum of money and made some life-changing promises if his friend could help get the shop from its owner. The entrusted friend paid the manager a visit, in which he started a conversation to examine the man's determination regarding the situation of leasing the premises. He discovered the manager was not ready to compromise and decided to try to lure him into the lion's den. He noticed that the manager was tired after long hours of working and suggested that he employ a young man to do the job because, after all, the manager was getting older and all he needed to do was pay the younger employee wages.

"Oh, you are right! What a nice idea," the manager replied.

"I'll find you a strong man," the friend replied.

Just a few weeks later, while the manager was resting, some health and environmental officers came to inspect the shop. When his attention was called to a problem, he found it difficult to take matters seriously and thought it would be a waste of time for the inspectors. To his surprise, he saw some dead rats and different kinds of insects all around the kitchen, and enough evidence to establish the fact the shop hadn't be kept tidy for a long time.

Just then, his new best friend walked into the shop pretending to pay him a visit and was speechless at the sight of the dirty kitchen. While the environmental officers were taking pictures and making recordings as part of their evidence report, a white van filled with immigration officers pulled up in front of the shop. Seeing that, the new young worker jumped out through the window and ran. The manager couldn't believe he had been involved in illegal employment. What a mess! He wanted to verify the worker's passport but his friend discouraged him, and the situation became a double tragedy.

Following due process, the business premises were sealed up by the local authorities and a huge fine was levied on him by the immigration authorities. In the week following, the manager tried to get over his troubles and carry on. However, pictures taken by the environmental officers of what was found in their inspection were placed in more than three leading daily newspapers, with headlines such as, "The rat and chips shop," "The mysteries of the chips legend," and "Dead rat in the chips tower." Various articles were published on the need for local residents to be mindful of what type of food they buy and consume.

With every effort the manager made to raise the bar at his place of business, there were obstacles from every direction. His friend advised him to bribe an official to help turn the situation toward his favor, but the following day pictures of him giving money to the officials were published in the dailies and issues leaped from the frying pan into the fire. At the next meeting with the local authorities, to which he was accompanied by his good friend, the officials decided to seal the business premises indefinitely and revoke his business license because his actions were about to cast the authorities' reputations in disrepute.

While the manager was deciding whether to appeal the decision or not, some local residents sued him in court for selling poisonous meals to them while the business was in operation. Some members of the public petitioned the local authorities for not making the manager render a public apology, which he refused at first because he was actually innocent of all charges. However, his friend advised him to stand up as a leader who takes full responsibility for his mistakes.

During this disruptive period, he forgot to pay the immigration service fine and was made to appear in court, which increased his debt. Everything that had gone wrong would have broken the back of even the strongest man. Due to high legal fees and other forms of pressure, the manager had to auction his building to a young lady who claimed to be a property developer, inasmuch as the business had lost its integrity in the public's sight, making his situation similar to that of those who lost everything, whom the sun used to laugh at their yard. As Jackie Chan said in *The Karate Kid* movie, "When life knocks you down, you have the choice either to fight back or give it up."

Having learned from his mistakes, the courageous manager left the community to set up another business elsewhere. A few weeks later, he discovered that the rich man had accomplished his mission and wondered how he was able to buy the premises, but the ex-manager decided to let go of his previous situation. It was sometime later, during a misunderstanding between the rich man and his best friend, that the cat was let out of the bag. The young man who worked in the shop and was assumed to be an illegal resident was, in fact, a benefice citizen of that particular country and was one of the rich man's aides. He had used a fake passport to hide his real identity, which the "best" friend was aware of. What a strategic trap!

However, it was later discovered that the local authority officer was just a student who was hired to frame him and fuel matters against him. The young lady who was disguised to be an auctioneer was the personal assistant to the rich man. The issue was that the rich man wasn't he able to start his fast food business as he wished until he was able to soil the integrity of the family business and thus bringing it down. The rich man knew the secret of which the family business was built on before making it his major target. He knew what he wanted and gave it his all, but it cost him due to the carelessness and ignorance of the manager who opened the door for his adversity. The business that was built on integrity was also brought down through its integrity. The manager later made it up the ladder of success based on his business experience. But losing the shop, which was considered to be the family's heritage, brought shame that he would never forget for the rest of his life. The good news was that the rich man never fulfilled his promise to his friend but called him a betrayer. This made him isolate himself from the same friend, but the situation was a medicine after death, which is no longer applicable and reasonable. Only if he had not taken his friend's advice, he wouldn't have lost the business on the grounds of a damaged reputation, also the building he valued and lost would still be in his possession. As a common African proverb states, *"While my enemy remains in my backyard, my foe abides within my household"*. One vital fact of life which is true is that friends are good because they keep one away from loneliness, but they would only suggest to you what to buy but never pay the fee at the point of transaction, and if a friend would have to lend you, you might have to pay double. The painful part of the whole story was that before the truth of the matter was revealed, the serious damages had already been done and could not be amended because integrity was what the business stood for and the same was used in pulling it down.

Without integrity, a man cannot be valued by others. Integrity is about considering others before one's personal interests and it's one of the major characteristics of an effective leader. Integrity is also about a person's beliefs, words, and actions. Some leaders' beliefs are deceitful, mostly in the world of politics, whereby huge promises are made before politicians are elected to public offices and once there, the game changes. However, most politicians like this are either voted out or forced out of office in a humiliating manner. A man of integrity always abides by his words and is not inconsistent nor offers excuses once they attain the office they sought. Some leaders do seek to renegotiate or redesign their platform after an agreement has been reached, but people of integrity always think before acting or making promises in order to avoid situations that question their creditability. Integrity is about facing the reality in all we do at any point in time in aligning our action towards achieving our desires, imagine a single lady wishing to get married and not taking care of herself or the young man seeking a job and not making out an application either online or by post.

In a nutshell, integrity needs to be seen as a way of life and a character bond which enables the world to be a better place. According to Michelle Obama, wife of the first African-American president of the United States of America, "We learned about honesty and integrity—that the truth matters; that you don't take shortcuts or play by your own set of rules. Success doesn't count unless you earn it fair and square. "According to Michelle's quote, the truth matters in anything worth doing. Without the truth, a legacy can never last. The truth is rarely smooth and never simple, but without it, no man can be identified with integrity. The only thing that sets a man free is the truth because it's about saying and doing what's right and expected. The point is that anyone who wants to be identified with integrity needs to truthful, not basing his actions on *authentic statements or facts* i.e. similar to the truth but not actually the truth. The truth in a man facilitates others to trust him and once well-known for it, better opportunities look for such a man while others might have to struggle for the same opportunity.

I remember the story of a former chief executive of an oil and gas company who was forced out of office by some political godfathers for refusing to make the so-called "returns," i.e. 'cooking the books 'of the company and paying an unaccounted for sum of money to the godfather for no good reason. The funniest part of the matter is that the rule of the game was, if caught, 'you walk alone'. In other words, if the chief executive is caught in the act of corruption, he dances alone to the music. Long story short, nemeses later caught up with political godfathers after power was taken over by another political party which exposed their irregularities; some of the godfathers were jailed, while some committed suicide due to the high level of disgrace. It is commonly said that honesty is the best policy, the chief executive was later appointed as the minister for oil and gas resources in the same country due to record.

Professionals in the financial, medical, and legal world need to be more aware of the importance of truthfulness in all their relationships with the general public by avoiding deceitfulness or misunderstanding because their services are very vital for the sake of humanity.

Integrity is a challenging quality of leadership and life as a whole because it's only meant for the strong-minded and never the weak one, to remain standing in both rain or shine for what is true and right. Many do wisely go for the alternative ways of doing things simply because it's not harmful or could be referred to as good but the truth's efforts stand the test of time, reality, and value. This book explains the basic facts of integrity in all aspects of daily life; it consists of interesting stories to reflect upon concerning the need for being reliable, honest, and content in life.

INTRODUCTION

In recent times, there has been a lot of discussion about the lack of integrity in many areas of both private and public life. It is of special concern in areas such as politics, economics, business, journalism, the media, and even in today's religious world. It is often discussed in a psychological and moral sense. There must be integrity within as well as beyond all areas of life. According to William (Bill) Barry who once said: "There is no shortcut to becoming a person of wisdom and integrity.It is a journey, not a destination because the journey continues as far as we live." According to Brenda Walsh and Racine Dominican in their article: "We live in a culture that is saturated with false gods and distractions of every kind. People are faced with a smorgasbord of choices in the media and there are few guideposts to lead people to make choices that reflect a life of integrity. The call of the Spirit within often gets drowned out by the noise, clutter, and temptations of our day. We need integrity in our inner life and outer life in order to claim we are living with integrity."

A world without integrity would be referred to as a lawless, manipulative, and inconsequential state. It's also referred to as a situation of no value or reputation, where nothing works for the betterment of all. A world without integrity is a world that lacks morality. It's a world of cheaters in any government and other offices of public trust that gets off the hook and fosters partiality, not equality. However, all sweet things must eventually come to end, the upright might look stupid in a corrupted state but the long arm of the law caught up with unjust mercies which become silver, while favor becomes golden. Those hailing then later come to pity them. The major fact which people need to understand is holding that leadership, political, or any other public office should be seen as a platform to serve others with humility and transform the society in a positive way, not for the purpose of enriching themselves, boosting an inferiority complex or depriving others of what could have benefited their lives. To those occupying top or strategic offices at present, they should bear in mind the adage "What goes around comes around"; for no one would be in power forever and records would always tell the truth. Those in top positions in government any other organization would be always be remembered for something either positive or negative. If anyone should aim at enriching themselves as the reason for holding public offices, such is a failure just like the bulldozer's father whose son reaped what he sowed. Barack Obama, the first black American president of the United States, will never be forgotten in the history of America due to his ability to connect with most of the youths by reducing the student loan interest rate and dramatically changing the healthcare laws, to count a few. A world without integrity is a state where dishonesty and corruption take the lead of the day and become an established culture. A world without integrity is a state where there is no regard for the law, and laws are made by the few for the inconvenience of the many. It's a world of deceit, lack of responsibility, and broken promises. The gospel truth is, until something is done, nothing changes in terms of someone taking the lead in doing what is right and acceptable.

I once trusted a friend to help me get some first-class stamps and post an application, so I gave him some money and went on another mission. To my surprise, a few weeks later I discovered he posted the application with a second-class stamp. Through his careless handling of the receipt, which he told me he misplaced, he requested more money because he claimed he added more money of his own to make the application an express post. When I showed him the receipt and asked why he had behaved in such a manner, he replied, "Oh, life is a game and one needs to be smart." Oh? What a lovely idea! Furthermore, he told me, "If you don't play people, someone would play you and dump you". I then understood why I needed to give him the red card because his perception about life is of no integrity. However, he saw no reason, to be honest in anything worth doing. I feel sorry for his family, workplace, and the social clubs he might belong to because he who lacks integrity tends to also lack morality and self-respect to behave in an acceptable manner and such people are well known to be smart in smuggling for what is good for themselves and not others.

A particular fact of life my old friend had forgotten is that one bad apple can spoil the bunch, and people only want to do business and associate with people they trust. That's certainly how I feel up to this very day. The fact is, without integrity, no one can create a positive and lasting impact in the lives of others and no man leaves a better legacy without integrity. A man who is not consistent in his words and actions will likely never be regarded as dignified or authentic in his relationship with others. Such inaction would not be seen as integrity because integrity requires personal discipline, trustworthiness, credibility, and endurance to make one's life worthwhile.

According to Steven W. Vannoy, "Integrity is how you act when no one is watching. It's always telling the truth, clearing up misconceptions or partial truths. It's never knowingly hurting anybody or anything. Integrity is keeping commitments." Webster's Third International Dictionary defines integrity as "an uncompromising adherence to a code of moral, artistic, or other values; utter sincerity, honesty, and candor, avoidance of deception, expediency, artificiality, or shallowness of any kind". This definition requires sacrifice to attain the level of being identified as having integrity and not being "smart" like my unfaithful friend. It takes men of integrity to change an organization or community because they would have to pass the test of trust and quality to be distinguished and considered reliable. However, the words, actions, and decisions made or taken by men with integrity are greatly respected and taken seriously. Leadership without integrity is meaningless and irrelevant, nothing more and end of story. Integrity needs to be maintained within all aspects of life. Once mistrust occurs at any point it could cause problems against once previous performance in the long run. In the cooperate world, lack of integrity could lead to financial losses, embezzlement of funds, job losses, and organizational structure starting to unravel.

Integrity has a lot to do with the effective performance and success required to keep an organization in good standing and able to edge out competitors. One of the vital aspects an organization needs to take seriously is customer service because it deals with ensuring that products are of the expected standard and price in which customers are ready to purchase, therefore enabling them to remain loyal to the organization. Integrity occurs when each member of an organization or a team does what is right and expected of them at the right time. Leaders with integrity keep the hope of a bright future alive in their followers because integrity is the highest currency a leader ever needs to carry. From my experience as a life coach, whenever an honest leader communicates a vision to others, it's easy to see the big picture because the honesty attitude in such leaders radiates light for the vision to look authentic and reliable. In the business world and everyday life, personal integrity is critical for getting and keeping the support of our loved ones and well-wishers. Likewise, an organization's integrity is critical for getting and keeping customers and suppliers, because future success depends on doing the right thing and once a man or an organization is well known as having integrity, opportunities find him without him having to search for them.

However, the need to live and lead with integrity can't be underestimated; because people always want to follow leaders they believe in and trust beyond a reasonable doubt to get them where they want to be. Integrity is one of the concepts of consistency in terms of actions, values, methods, measures, principles, expectations, and outcomes. It expresses a deep commitment towards doing the right thing for the right reason at the right time, regardless of the circumstances. Embracing integrity as a way of life always facilitates personal growth because it goes along with constant learning and understanding of how to get things done in the right manner. Another outcome of embracing integrity as a way of life is the tendency of being identified as reliable, i.e. sticking with problems and issues until they are resolved from a win/win point of view and strong consideration for all stakeholders involved which reflects effectiveness. Purposeful leading is always a result of embracing integrity i.e. without compromising standards.

John Maxwell hammered this home in one of his write-ups: "When you follow the Golden Rule and live with integrity, you set an example that has a far greater impact than any words you could ever speak. Why is leading by example such a powerful concept? I can answer that with five short words: People do what people see." Integrity is all-encompassing, it's not something you demonstrate at home or when in a social or professional gathering. People of integrity don't live bifurcated lives; their morals, ethics, treatment of others, and overall character are the same wherever they are, whatever they're doing. In a nutshell, people of integrity are known to be consistent and stable in all they do.

I would like to make some critical viewpoints of how the various components of integrity work. These can be referred to as reasonable and applicable laws which enable one to become a person identified with the value to influence others without the use of force. For better understanding, integrity is not perfection, because it involves being willing to admit one's mistakes where necessary as well as learning from and loving others, even when they seem unlovable. In reality, integrity can't be attained by force, because it's a matter of treating others the same way you would like to be treated.

Essentially, integrity is a matter of getting things done with all sincerity, i.e. without any form of pretense, deceit, or hypocrisy. The story of Ananias and Sapphira in the Bible is a good example of why things need to be done with all sincerity. The book of Acts, Chapter 5, gives an accurate account of why trust is a vital element in any relationship because both Ananias and Sapphira had good intentions of doing what was right, but they did things in an unacceptable manner. I am sure that if only they were sincere in their relationship, they would have been recognized and regarded as icons in the Christian faith, such as Moses, Solomon, and others. Bear in mind, a legacy founded on integrity always remains relevant and realistic, because one good turn always deserves another. Integrity is the best way of life; it enables a leader to influence others to act in a particular direction without the use of force or authority. Once a leader loses his integrity he becomes a pen without ink, a toothless lion or bulldog, or in most cases a blunt knife. The only platform needed to live a life of integrity is the desire to live and lead purposefully, which enables one to become a person of significance. It's quite understandable as human's that making mistakes at one point or another in our lives is inevitable. Therefore, we have to seek smart alternatives in getting things done. We are sometimes lucky to have made our way before being trapped in the hole, yet we still need to ensure things are done as expected. Some do purposefully misbehave for selfish reasons and they end up paying by losing more than they've gained in doing less than what was expected of them. Some misbehave due to mounted pressure, influence base on relationship with some who might end up not caring if you found yourself in *deep waters* or due to the fear of failure, either the first time or more, in which one might be trying to avoid but the fact is it's better one does what is right than getting oneself into trouble either knowingly or unknowingly while trying to be nice or helpful to others because ignorance of the law is no excuse. Herman Melville, the American novelist once said during his lifetime *"It is better to fail in originality than to succeed in imitation".* I strongly believe in this principle because to the mature-minded, failure is never a final destination but a platform for learning and improvement. The beauty of a man's life could only be reflected when he fails and tries again still he succeeds in his endeavor.

WHY INTEGRITY?

"In all things showing yourself to be a pattern of good works; in doctrine showing integrity, reverence, incorruptibility."

Titus 2:7

No matter how educated, talented, rich, or coolheaded a man might believe he is, how he sees and treats others reflects everything about him because the fact is integrity is everything. Integrity is not about knowing it in terms of words written with paper and ink, but the real understanding in practical terms. Integrity is measured in one's relationships with others under any and every situation. If all leaders could have only one quality, it should be integrity. Character-wise, integrity is the quality of being above reproach, true to one's word, and not compromising the right principles even when under fire. Leaders who believe and understand what integrity is in its real context always see and treat others equally. They act responsibly by doing what they promise to do and not making excuses. In a world of integrity, all people need to be seen as equal and not regarding some better than others.

Integrity reflects everything about a man and proves beyond a reasonable doubt that what a man does when trusted with great responsibility is what is right in every circumstance. Integrity is a core aspect of effective leadership because it's established on right thinking, exhibiting the right attitude, and positively affecting others around us. Brian Tracy, one of the most respected success experts in the world once said: "leaders with integrity aren't afraid of the truth". This is called the reality principle of seeing the world as it really is not as you wish it to be. It is perhaps the most important principle of leadership and it determines one's level of worthiness because it demands truthfulness and honesty. He went on further by saying that "Many companies and organizations fail because they don't follow the reality principle of integrity which means telling the truth even if the truth is ugly and bitter, it's better, to be honest than to delude others because you are probably deluding yourself too".

For a better understanding, integrity is the condition or quality of being complete, undivided, or unbroken. It's an unimpaired condition, a moral soundness or uprightness in any given situation. Integrity means following your moral and ethical convictions and doing the right thing in all circumstances, even if no one is watching you. Being of integrity means you are true to yourself and would do nothing that demeans or dishonors you. The pure fact of living or leading with integrity is never an easy task; it's about ignoring advice on how to cheat others, including the payment of taxes without getting caught. It's about keeping confidential information to yourself and only passing it on to the right people at the right time.

According to Alan Cohen: "You are in integrity when the life you are living on the outside matches who you are on the inside." In reality, acting with integrity reflects the real intentions of a man in terms of how consistent and competent he is in whatever right thing he does. It is about having the courage to say "no" if asked to bend the rules for selfish interests, i.e. deception and expediency. It's about having the courage to face the truth in a fearless manner and doing the right thing that is accepted and expected by all.

Embracing a lifestyle of integrity requires living a life where your actions are aligned with your beliefs and not those of someone else. Trying to succeed according to someone else's standards will wear you down and get you nowhere. According to Bernard Baruch, the American financier and stock investor said: *"Be who you are and say what you feel, because those who mind don't matter, and those who matter don't mind"*. Forcing someone into a box created by others makes life difficult and it leads to negative consequences at one point or another. When we cultivate a lifestyle based on integrity, it enables us to unlock our determination, focus more on what gives inspiration in overcoming limitations and enable us to go the extra mile which is a parameter towards being distinguished.

As was commonly said way back in my school days: "There is dignity in all labor, but the reality is there is dignity only in labor with integrity".

Integrity is not creating barriers to bar people from growth and other opportunities, i.e. when a leader claims to believe and invest in a person (the greatest asset of any organization) but then refuses to develop them for advancements not placing a limit on the extent they could attain. This is a major cause of failure in leadership in the long run.

I would like to share the story of the acting manager who was assigned to manage a project alongside his team members. Due to the distance and logistics involved, it was agreed that the acting manager would lodge the team members in a nearby bed and breakfast hotel. It was also agreed that he should hire a hoist for the lifting of heavy materials for the team's health and safety. The estimated cost was submitted and approved by the company's financial director. On arrival at the project destination, the manager kept his team members waiting, only to return with two second-hand shipping containers. The team members were shocked and they questioned his action because this was a change from the previous talks, but he misleads them by claiming the hotel had been fully booked, except for the remaining room which he booked for himself. In addition, he never hired a hoist but made the team members carry heavy materials for a long time, which lessened the expected efficiency and effectiveness in the long run. However, he threatened to sack anyone found calling the head office, as all questions should be directed to him.

After a few days on the project, a team member overheard a telephone conversation in which the manager told the project director that he would be in need of more money to settle the hotel bill because the low-cost rooms were fully booked and he had to take more expensive rooms for his team members. Unbeknownst to him, pictures of the second- handed shipping containers had been sent to the executive director via email. The director ordered an investigation and made the team members stay close to him to bear witness to his conversation in which the team had decided to take the risk of recording him. To his surprise, the project director, whom he had tomislead, arrived at the project site without noticing the time. The project director degraded him by visiting the shipping containers he tricked his team members into staying in and was ashamed of the manager. He then called the manager in and asked him to explain how the health and safety conditions he claimed to have met according to the report he sent to the head office and demanded a refund for the money that was paid into his account by the finance director. When he no longer got answers to his questions, the manager was instructed to leave the site, to report at the head office, and one of the senior team members was assigned to take over the project. This man was never allowed to return to the workplace; I am sure he would be ashamed to tell his family why he left the job unexpectedly. If he had only understood and embraced integrity, he would have been in peace and harmony with his team members and the management of the company. He would have been confirmed as a full manager at the completion of the project, but only if he had acted honestly, which was the case of the team member who took over his post. Without a doubt, none of the stakeholders of the company wanted to associate themselves with the former manager for any reason because he violated the precepts of integrity. Apart from being confirmed as a full manager, he would have made his way to becoming one of the directors, because he was running postgraduate study at the time he misbehaved. There was something essential he had yet to understand—that integrity is a vital element of leadership, and stakeholders at one point or another act or speak out to challenge decisions and actions that lack integrity in any sphere of life.

Unfortunately, integrity has no meaning to many people, because they don't understand what it means in terms of its rewards. An average man's opinions and choices are usually based on the popularity of particular politicians, which is always influenced by negative reports from the media. Unfortunately, some media reports are paid for by corrupt politicians and so-called godfathers who struggle for public office by tricking the general public for their own selfish interests and not the common good. The sad fact is that the civilized world gives bogus awards such as honorary doctorates and distinguished medals at various public events to those who were never held accountable for stewardship while in office. They are commonly rewarded for their charitable work and good causes. The fact is they get rewarded for favoring certain stakeholders behind closed doors and made use of the media to elevate themselves. It is shameful when the poor hail them for their undisciplined acts and make them role models.

A king's name whose reign brought peace and harmony is never forgotten in his land because his legacy always lives on. In order for integrity tobe established in today's world, stakeholders need to be willing and ready to stand and fight for the future benefits by thinking and acting right, and not seeking current and immediate gains in a selfish manner or giving up their rights and future entitlements in exchange for a bowl of porridge like that of Esau and Jacob.

Many years ago, two young politicians were contending for the post of the local authority chairperson. Both were children of retired local councilors who had served the local authority some twenty years earlier. As Election Day was drawing near, stakes and expectations grew higher and various promises were being made on both sides. In light of a narrow media election poll, the community youth association decided to organize a public debate at the town hall. After the first round, they challenged each other by questioning the other opponent about their credibility and ability to govern the local council effectively. Mr. A., who called himself 'the political bulldozer', questioned Mr. B., who called himself 'the evergreen legacy', his opponent what the terms politics, government, public policy, and leadership meant. He also claimed Mr. B. was a political novice. Mr. B. responded as follows, "Thank you very much, Mr. Mentor", he began. "If I needed to learn what is meant by politics, government, and leadership, it would not be the son of the most wanted and corrupt politician in the history of the nation. I hope you did not learn the terms accountability and integrity from your father while he was in office because his inability to understand those terms made him involve himself in the misappropriation of public funds, which made him spend over ten years in self-imposed exile when the long arm of the law was after him." I wished he had waited to prove his innocence of the allegation leveled against him. "Sir, are you aware that he who clothe his fellow man would simply be judged by the clothes he is putting on?" He asked Mr Bulldozer.

At that point, Mr. A. began to feel uncomfortable and started to lose his temper, because his family, including his biological father and other "godfathers" who had invested heavily in expectation for huge returns, were all in the audience and their initial smiles were no longer visible. He then shouted that Mr. B. had told lies, and responded, "Show your proof." Mr. B. then opened his file and brought out documents showing the misappropriation of funds made by Mr. A.'s father while in office. In addition, he showed copies of newspapers with pictures of his father with damaging headlines and reports declaring him a wanted man. Mr. B. proceeded to ask Mr. A. if his father appeared at the police station and court for hearings on the allegations leveled against him and if he could prove that his bulldozing was not for the purpose of digging deep into what his father did before running from the long arm of the law. Furthermore, Mr. B. asked his counterpart if his father's legacy had stood the test of time, value, and reality, and what assurance was there that digging deeper wouldn't create even more evidence against his father? Mr. B. claimed that he was proud of his own late father's legacy and said he decided to step into politics to uphold his father's honest legacy.

Mr. A. could not respond and left the debate venue in an awful mood, which gave Mr. B. an edge in winning the election unopposed. By then it was too late for Mr. A's party to redeem his image in the public's eyes, which made his money useless, and there was no time to choose another candidate to run for the post. The fact is, Mr. A. lost the election before it even started because his foundation was in trouble and there was nothing he could do about it. His father's legacy couldn't help him because it lacked the vital element of leadership which is known as integrity.

The need to live with integrity is vital. Integrity means our lives are in alignment with what is right. The world would be a better place to live if we all became courageous enough to speak up and stand for the truth in a fearless manner, even at a cost to ourselves. When we practice integrity, our lives will be based on truth and justice for all. In reality, integrity is a quality that is often talked about in connection with leadership but is not always easy to define. It includes honesty, decency, ethics, authenticity, and uprightness in everything we do. A profession or a world without justice and integrity is just a state of commotion.

Public administration is another area where integrity is expected at its highest level. Public authorities must behave appropriately in their dealings with citizens, businesses, and other public authorities, both locally and internationally. Office holders, elected representatives, appointed or public servants must behave professionally and ethically in the interest of integrity. They must not commit fraud, accept bribes, or leak confidential information in exchange for anything in order to set themselves as a role model for the younger generation. This book consists of essential acts of integrity which are the vital qualities required to make one's life and leadership style worth embracing by others. Abiding by the acts discussed in this book would make one relevant, distinguished, and a person of substance.

Taking deep insights from the book of Proverbs in the Bible, integrity is a vital quality that gives a man lasting peace, because it means living one's life with credibility. Proverbs 20:7 says, "A righteous man who walks in his integrity, How blessed are his sons after him." The mystery behind this passage is that once a man lays integrity as a foundation for his children, greatness will eventually become their heritage. It takes a deep understanding of integrity to think twice before acting because every recent action becomes history afterward. **Proverbs 22:1** reads: **"A good name is rather to be chosen than great riches." Proverbs 19:1** makes it clear: **"Better is a poor man who walks in his integrity than he who is perverse in speech and is a fool."** To clear the air, integrity is about fighting and championing a good cause for the benefit of others and not playing smart for selfish interests. Men of integrity talk and also walk in and out. However, being a man of wisdom and intelligence can be only be attained while doing what is right.

People of integrity are constantly looking for ways to grow, which often makes them excellent in leading others because it earns them a better recognition after a while. In leading others, leaders could endeavor to listen to others and not just dominating them. According to Andy Stanley, *Leaders who refuse to listen will eventually be surrounded by people who have nothing significant to say.* In a nutshell, a leader needs to be straightforward in their relationship with others because if there is any level of deceit, pretense, or cover-up, the truth will eventually catch up and once the cat is out of the bag, mighty icons can fall. People who believe in integrity never consider taking shortcuts or playing by their own set of rules simply because they're in a position to determine who goes or comes, what falls or rises, or simply because no one is watching. The fact is accountability is above anyone, and it goes along with abiding by the laws of common sense.

I remember that as an accounting student in college, getting the final answer is not the major issue in solving any accounting question. What mattered was following the required steps to arrive at the right answer. Following the right steps reflects your knowledge and understanding about the problem you are solving. Achieving success or excellence is good, but it needs to be earned in a fair and right manner, i.e. not blackmailing someone else to achieve it. In soccer, every time the ball enters the net does not necessarily count as a goal because the ball could be an offside or a handball. The integrity of the game needs to be maintained for the sake of interested stakeholders. Bear in mind, no one is interested in listening to a man with a tarnished personality talk less of people following him. Leadership without integrity is totally worthless. Men who believe in and live with integrity are always inwardly fulfilled. They are happy with whatever they have and experience real peace of mind.

One major quality of those who embrace integrity is that they are lovers of the truth. The telling of the truth is essential, not bending it in the name of diplomacy. They see integrity as a way of life and as an act of authenticity because it reflects the real personality of a man. People of integrity don't speak or take action when they're not sure of the facts in a given situation. They would rather work hard to investigate an issue before commenting on it. People of integrity act in a straightforward, consistent manner that is not controversial. They do not pretend to be something they are not. They take responsibility for their actions and also admit their mistakes without making excuses or blaming those around them for failure. They consider failure to be an opportunity to learn from their mistakes, to improve themselves and be better prepared for the next opportunity. They see any form of criticism as constructive and as a platform for improvement. They study the feelings of others before formulating policies in order to minimize conflict among organizational stakeholders.

According to Zig Zigler, "The most important persuasion tool you have in your entire arsenal is integrity." The way to become a successful leader is to embody trustworthiness and honesty. Integrity is critical for those who rely on persuasion to achieve their objectives. A reputation for integrity makes it easier for others to follow a leader because subordinates have learned to have a higher degree of trust in such people. The absence of truth makes it hard to persuade others in the effective execution of a plan, and lack of trust is the fastest track to failure.

Leaders with integrity are often known to be humble and respectful, which enables them to remain connected, committed, sincere, and working in collaboration with others. These qualities make communication easier and more effective in achieving goals. Another notable characteristic of leaders with integrity is their ability to help others succeed without playing the role of 'I am the boss' in any situation. Leaders see the need to develop others and encourage them to share the spotlight for the sake of growth and improvement. According to John Maxwell, "Leadership is about helping others to be smarter than they are, not leaders being smarter than their team members."

THE ACT OF ACCOUNTABILITY

"The right thing to do and the hard thing to do are usually the same."

Steve Maraboli

In simple, common sense terms accountability can be regarded as the fact or condition of being accountable and responsible for one's action in any given situation. Accountability is the guiding principle that defines how commitments are carried out by various stakeholders within an organization. Accountability is a measure of reporting the outcome of an event in relationship to situations for strategic purposes. In a nutshell, accountability is essential in measuring progress attained during an operation to avoid wasting resources.

When we take a critical view of some the world's biggest financial scandals that ever occurred, companies such as Enron and WorldCom will never be forgotten in the financial history. Enron kept huge debts off the balance sheet in 2002 and went on to present fudged accounting statement to its stakeholders. All was well until an internal whistleblower brought it to air. Another was at World.com, in which the internal auditing department uncovered a total of $3.8 billion in fraud and inflated its revenues with fake accounting entries. Both organizations were heavily fined, had their chief executives who were the key players' fired in which two of the three ended up serving jail sentences. The fact is their selfish act lead to the loss of jobs and affected families in a negative way. The key players would have done away with it but the principle of accountability fished out their wrong doings. One of the serious principles of corporate life is Accountability, which demands the board of an organization to communicate to the company's shareholders and other stakeholders, at regular intervals a fair, balanced and understandable assessment of how it's achieving its business purpose and meeting its other responsibilities. Accountability cannot be said to exist in situations where judgment and sanction do not operate. The need for sanction arises because it is in the general interest that useful actions be encouraged and their opposite discouraged. Application of sanction to acts of authority forms part of the conditions essential for accountability.

Mahatma Gandhi, a man who believed in fairness, once said, "It is wrong and immoral to seek to escape the consequences of one's acts." I read an online account of a former government minister who sought godfathers to intercede on her behalf after her term in office. I am sure her conscience had begun to bother her because if she had no skeletons in her closet, there would be no reason to cover up anything relating to her service for the government. The truth is she knew it was the end of Christmas and accountability would be expected of their stewardship. I imagine that when she was in office, she saw herself as invincible, forgetting that no man or woman is above the state and that a time would come when she would be questioned about her conduct while in office. A man who understands what integrity is would never be afraid of being held accountable for his actions, especially when placed in a position of money, influence, and power which reflects his trustworthiness.

Another woman who once served in the British government in a high office was about to be made a baroness, but the British public considered her unfit due to her role in the monetary controversies during her term in office. One must understand the full meaning of integrity to hold onto its values and never compromise them. Accountability is about making a commitment to respond to and balance the needs of stakeholders in a company's decision-making. However, effective leaders don't blame others; rather, they accept responsibility in light of poor performance or outcome. They also take responsibility and courage toward fixing the problem and learning from the experience, which is a better platform for improvement. In leadership, accountability is the acknowledgment of responsibility for actions, products or outcomes, administration, governance, and implementation of strategies. The fact is and still remains that without accountability there's no leadership. Leadership without accountability can lead to failure because if a sense of purpose is not identified with mutually agreed-upon goals and the requisite platform to provide regular performance feedback things would go astray.

Accountability also encompasses the obligation of reporting, explaining, and answering to one's stewardship in a true and fair manner. Accountability needs to be carried out in a way that stands the test of time, value, and quality because without these three elements it can't be regarded as being authentic. Accountability is a personal willingness to answer for the results of one's behaviors and actions regardless of how things turn out. Accountability also has a strong connection to stakeholders' expectations. Performance-wise, those finding it difficult to meet targets need to be supported in order to meet stakeholders' expectations. However, they must also be able to defend their stewardship, because investors and other stakeholders are not interested in excuses. I would like to share the story of the dishonest journalist who was recommended and assigned to make a particular coverage during the war period in a well-known country by a particular international community. The coverage was required as a result of the high level of petitions made by various international and local organizations regarding the entrusted organization's inability to supply good food and water to the displaced. The organization had not been delivering what was agreed upon and suspected that they and some top politicians had influenced a lot of manipulation and misappropriation of funds. However, at the conclusion of the coverage and investigation, less damage than reported was observed based on the video clips and written report by the smart journalist. A few days after the speech of the community representative, another petition was made regarding the underestimation of the situation and in the light of social media; posted images were unbelievable by every stakeholder. However, the cameraman was invited to explain what he understood of the video clip that was submitted by the smart journalist. The cameraman denied the video clip and tendered his copy which the smart journalist thought he had destroyed and there was no trace of evidence that could be used against the seemingly guilty parties. Unknown to everyone, the camera used had an internal recording device. After the situation became clear as the day, it was later discovered that the smart journalist had played ball with the same politicians causing chaos. They paid him to fabricate his report and gave a recorded video clip to tender with his report. The one who recommended him was highly disappointed and he was sentenced to two years in jail for his dishonesty on the grounds he misleads the public and he acted without any form of integrity.

In leadership, accountability only becomes realistic with reasonable expectations. This was the case of the story of the talents in the Bible i.e. **Matthew 25:14-30.** "It was recorded that the master allocated to each servant according to their ability, which he knew based on their performance, and he had reasonable expectations before the allocation of the talents. However, on the day of accountability, he rewarded each according to his performance without any form of cheating."

Having a reasonable expectation is vital in every stewardship situation regardless of the size of the organization. However, it's up to every leader to have a clear understanding of what is expected of them within a specific period. This enables team members to understand their roles and operate within the expected scope of responsibility. Without this understanding, it would be difficult to influence and carry on their team, and performance could suffer a setback as a result. It's paramount to be inquisitive, ask questions, and engage people in conversation. A leader needs to listen and solicit feedback to identify and eliminate whatever might cause a setback in terms of meeting targets. Accountability is about having the required intellectual ability to meet expectations. It's important to effectively plan for the unknown by identifying potential problems, mutually understanding their consequences, and to take pre-emptive action to avoid them from occurring. In understanding what accountability is in practical terms, the impact of team performance cannot be ignored. The fact is, nothing else reflects how capable and responsible one is other than what is commonly known as achievement, which is typically recorded in a performance evaluation. Greatness is never achieved alone, so effective leaders have to recognize the performance of those around them by promoting a culture of transparency. Another platform for promoting accountability is for leaders to be honest in their actions by instituting rewards and recognition for great performance. For purposes of accountability, a leader should never end a meeting without clarifying the next action steps for staff, such as the next performance review, and execution timelines and goals that are developed and committed to by following-up within a reasonable period of time.

To achieve better accountability, the need to establish trust and proper understanding within a team are critical. However, building teams to help translate plans into required action to implement an innovative culture facilitates better accountability. Such is the case with most football coaches because the teams place all of their expectations on the coach, regardless of player performance, therefore coaches have a higher stake, which makes them more accountable.

Organizations that focus more on accountability always find it easier to increase leads in a credible manner with stakeholders when they have a stronger governance structure and increased organizational learning processes. It is recommended that organizations embrace openness with their stakeholders about its activities and performance, provide them with basic information, financial statements, annual reports, and performance evaluations. Active participation is another aspect in accountability because it's important to consider the number and variety of stakeholders affected by any particular decision.

Responsibility is another aspect of accountability because there is nothing more frustrating than waiting longer than expected for a leader to respond to expected duties. A leader who lacks a sense of responsibility eventually finds trouble.

Responsibility tests whether a person is capable of owning up to accountability in any situation. In leadership, being responsible is important because it's a powerful platform for building trust in others.

It's paramount for everyone who wants to become an effective leader to demonstrate courage and responsibility in terms of remaining on course because once the act of taking responsibility is gone, nothing is easily achieved. Taking responsibility entails admitting one's mistakes in some cases, which doesn't make one a failure. Making mistakes isn't terrible if one is ready to learn from them and shows the courage and wisdom to continue once they are identified.

Considering responsibility in terms of accountability once again, important parameters need to be considered including the ability to identify the benefits of completing a task within the expected time frame, the ability to stay on course during the task and the ability to remain motivated until the successful completion of the project. Understanding what a leader is responsible for allows important insight to inspire others to achieve their goals. The unhidden fact is that after every task, accountability follows and the grace of making corrections becomes a medicine after death, which is a major reason why every leader needs to know how to establish and communicate standards of expected performance and behavior ahead of every task. According to Coach Bill-Parcells, *Individuals play the game, but teams win championships*. It's the responsibility of the leader to understand the right culture required for team members to remain on course towards achieving the expected.

Understanding accountability enables leaders to lead from the front and not by passing responsibility to team members and taking the glory later. However, achieving the best is another critical part of accountability as every stakeholder does have their expectations but it's up to every stakeholder to understand and embrace the organization's vision. There has to be an effective system of accountability within all levels of an organization. Both internal and external stakeholders need to be clear about their own level of input for things to have a better shape.

Sometimes things turn the other way around even when one has good intentions. Leaders need to research various ways of improving accountability to avoid things falling apart unexpectedly. In some cases, people get overloaded with responsibility while working under pressure. This can lead to frustration or loss of motivation in carrying out team duties as expected, which then lowers productivity. Apart from motivating or counseling team members, leaders need to know various ways to use effective communication by driving results to establish an accountability-based culture. This culture makes it easier to trace fault within an organization and to make reasonable adjustments before situations get out of control. It's also important for leaders to conduct follow-ups to review the performance of each team member to determine effectiveness and to share findings for the purpose of improvements. To sum it up on accountability, leadership shouldn't be all about what is in it for me but also the zeal to develop other leaders to attain a high level of effectiveness for growth in any situation. However, from experience, the fear of accountability is the reason why leaders in third world countries hold on to power, which leads to conflicts. They fail to realize that the long arm of the law, which is commonly known as the judicial authorities would hold them accountable for their actions and make them responsible for them. The problem is that many see power as a platform to enrich themselves and their loved ones while trying to avoid the consequences at the same time, the reality either dwell in a state of paradise or in a state of limbo we are all sojourners who needs to bear that no matter how sweet the journey, all sweet things would eventually have a limit, season and end.

THE ACT OF ACCESSIBILITY

"I certainly am interested in accessibility, clarity, and immediacy."

Paul Muldoon

In general, accessibility refers to the quality of being available when a leader is needed for a specific decision. In the business world, people like the accessibility of organizational customer service so they don't have to wait endlessly on hold to reach a human being who can help them resolve complaints. Another form of accessibility is being able to telephone an organization from any part of the world to make transactions, the internet has also become a prime method for accessing an organization from any point of the world.

There was a manager who was well known to be inaccessible, he was always reluctant to support his team members, and liked blaming others when an error occurs. Each quarter, whenever a performance review is conducted, his team was always the last in performance, which made his team members seek for transfer to other teams or departments within the organization and members of other teams do count themselves lucky not to be attached to him. While two of the company directors were about to step down, he was nominated to replace one the directors due to his years of service. Long story short, the company chairman decided to pay an unscheduled visit in which he found a member of the staff weeping at his mistake in handling one the machines because he would be penalized by the manager. The chairman, being an emphatic person, decided to accompany him to have a word with the manager, some other members of the staff informed the chairman that the manager was never an easy man and also backed it with instances. To the chairman's surprise, the manager had issued a suspension later without examining the situation. The chairman was shocked that decisions could be made with flexibility in which he considered not fair enough for the company's reputation. He then overruled the manager's decision because the situation wasn't intentional and the staff had shown remorse. Due to his inaccessible attitude, he wasn't recommended by the chairman to the shareholders for the position of a director at the following annual general meeting. He was frustrated and left the company.

Leaders with integrity should be physically present and make themselves accessible to their team members and stakeholders. To do this, leaders need to interact with and make themselves available to listen to employees, which show interest and participation. The act of being accessible enables leaders to adopt and maintain an "open door" policy to encourage the open flow of communication and maintain effective communication with stakeholders. Being accessible enables leaders to gain fast access to important information at appropriate times in order to make accurate strategic decisions.

As a life coach, I have come across ambitious people discussing huge dreams and visions. I do realize their dreams and visions are valuable and realistic which makes it attainable. The mistake most people with huge dreams and visions make is that they don't understand the difference between a vision and a mission. A vision is an idea or mental image of something at a particular time for a future purpose, while a mission is a task requires involvement if you are fulfilling a vision. In a few words, without embarking on a realistic mission, a vision remains unattainable. Another point is anyone whosoever cherishes his vision needs to take his mission serious because, it's the processes required in making a plan a reality and once a mission is in the state of chaos, the vision becomes unattainable. In a nutshell, vision is what we want to get done or achieve within a reasonable timeframe while missionis those things we need to do to achieve the vision. For example, soldiers go to war to win a battle, going to the battlefield is the mission, while winning the battle is their vision in which there are trained and prepared for. Anyone who wants to go miles in life would always require the support of others who are interested in his achievement. From experience, support is a form of sacrifice made by others around us in order to achieve, for a specific purpose, which needs to be meaningful to mankind. However, one could find it easy to carry a child or baby that stretches his arms i.e. those in need of support from others needs to be polite, humble, respectful and approachable in order to be seen as accessible. I have seen some people saying they would do it all alone, 'I would be fine', the fact such people need to understand is their chances of going far and doing more would always be limited, compromising the situation when they join forces with other like-minded people. Can you imagine an athlete competing in the 4 × 400 meters relay without the other three athletes and ended up winning the race? In reality, the athlete would have being tired before completing the second lap. The point is, individuals can only play the game but it takes effective teams to win. This is the reason why one needs to be accessible in order to agree, work and win with others. Another aspect of being accessible facilitates the ability to reason with others and not proving to be better than them. Being accessible enables us to appreciate and cherish one another and live happily, they're the cornerstone team dynamics and effectiveness within an organization. Some do believe they are reserved which is the reason not they don't associate themselves with others, however, few of those who do that make it a way of underestimating the efforts of others.

An important need for accessibility within an organization is to help eliminate potential barriers between leaders and others stakeholders. An effective leader isn't just such a figurehead whose picture is seen on a wall or website, but one who gets to know his or her team members in a context. It's also critical to acknowledge team members efforts, providing guidance when needed to help others to be a better version of themselves. From my experience, it requires one with positive thinking to become accessible to others. Positive thinkers see and approach a situation with an unbiased motive, they never act before matters occur but wait to see how things did towards achieving a positive outcome. In the context of reality, positive thinking reflects how humans could transform their approach to living so that humans can feel good about themselves, create worthwhile relationships and perform successfully. Another fact about positive thinking if applied regularly, it creates a positive lifestyle, environment, and enhances one's mood. On to hit it home on positive thinking, it create a platform to foresee the future lively, hopefully, and with authenticity rather than fear, hopelessness, and helplessness. In a community of positive thinkers, things work out fast for the betterment of everyone.

In reality, when discussing the future of an organization with relevant shareholders, one needs to be seen as being accessible with an open communication model before gaining the trust and commitment of stakeholders which could facilitate smooth relationships within an organization.

Many do believe in being strict and keeping away from others is the best way to reflect a high level of maturity and earn respect. The fact is most people who fall within the gap are believed to have less intellectual capability and confidence to relate with others and express themselves as expected. The bottom line is simple, to get it right you need the right people who are interested in knowing your idea or vision before investing in you. Those who fail in relating with the right people miss opportunities and never blame anyone for that but themselves alone. A man who never utilizes the best of any required opportunity can never be a role model to others because it takes an opportunity for a star to be made. A very good example is the x-factor which is a platform for people to showcase their talents and abilities in which people like Steve Brookstein, Shayne Ward, Leona Lewis, Joe McElderry, Matt Cardle and Little Mix were able to change the story of their lives. They were talented but x factor gave the opportunity to be a better version of themselves. However, some do pretend to be something they are not with the aim to cover up their weaknesses, but when reality exposes them, they do dislike themselves. Pretending is like living in another man's world in which there's no reward for. What a waste of time? As commonly said being gentle without being intelligent is equal to foolishness, because being accessible requires one to be intelligent and at the same time humble, according to Socrates the Greek philosopher, "I am the wisest man alive, for I know one thing, and that is that I know nothing." People who are accessible would hardly fail in any situation due to their ability to learn from others and not believing to know it all. According to Tony Buzan, learning how to learn is life's most important skill. In reality, a man who believes in learning would always experience improvement at various points in their life. Learning goes a long way in making positive efforts and just not awaiting results which be attained by any means which could end up being worthless on the long run.

One of the major reasons I respect the healthcare profession so much is its level of accessibility in the prevention of disease and disability. Keeping one's health stable creates the platform on which to improve the quality of life, prevention of untimely death, and to increase life expectancy. While addressing healthcare professionals, I discovered that part of the integrity required in this field is a need for more listening and making an accurate recording for the best decisions to be made. Timeliness is a vital aspect of healthcare because it represents the need to provide an effective service after a need is recognized. The ability to maintain a close working relationship is also a reflection of accessibility because it is a practical aspect of leadership, which involves connecting with others to have a good perception as a leader. It's a matter of smiling, feeling relaxed, and maintaining positive body language that enables others to feel comfortable while communicating.

It's paramount for leaders to let others know what they have achieved through hard work, and also to explain the impact of positive improvements in the future. As leaders become more successful, there are more demands made for their attention, which requires them not to only be physically present, but also accessible to handle challenges. When leaders are accessible, others see them with integrity and not fear. People trust and respect them, enabling solid relationships, allowing the team members to feel good about themselves, in turn reinforcing their own reputation and self-esteem. Accessibility is relating to others by being flexible and sticking to the principle of equality by avoiding the double standard game.

A friend of mine was a principal officer in one of the federal ministries in an African country. The government of the country embraced the initiative encouraging rail facilities to improve the transportation network. The ministry involved gave public notice for interested companies to tender offers in one of the dailies, publishing the required terms and conditions. After the deadline, the winning bid was announced at one of the fine hotels in the capital. After the winner was announced, some of the aggrieved parties and other stakeholders protested the decision, claiming lack of fairness and transparency in the differences in terms and conditions placed in the newspapers, compared to the one read at the public announcement. Upon investigation, it was discovered that the winner of the bid had a completely different version of the terms and conditions. In order to maintain integrity as promised, the chairman decided to suspend his decision and called for a quick meeting with officials behind closed doors. Upon further investigation, it was later revealed that the terms and conditions were changed by the secretary before mailing them to the press and the same secretary mailed the original copy to the announced winner. Furthermore, the secretary was a major shareholder in the company that won the bid, which she never declared before taking office.

The chairman walked her out of the event, disqualified the winner and awarded the job to the runner-up due to the company's financial soundness. The secretary had her appointment terminated and was made known on both digital and print news accounts, revealing her as an icon of mistrust and a person who lacked integrity. The bottom line is that integrity needs to be seen as the cornerstone of good governance in any establishment which requires the leader to be accessible and not playing a double standard game.

Leaders should be accessible before empowering others because they are skilled in the art of analysing situations in an unbiased manner before making decisions. From experience, I know that it is best to always be oneself, and it's also the easiest but not the most difficult thing to be is what other people want us to be. To relate with accessible leaders is the easiest way to keep an organization moving. Accessibility brings out leadership attributes in many leaders, such as the willingness to take reasonable risks for the sake of others and taking responsibility while others are making excuses. People who understand accessibility see the possibilities in tough situations while others see only the limitations. They courageously inspire others with a vision of what they can achieve for the better. However, the act of accessibility requires one to be realistic to avoid conflict and maintain his or her reputation. One must submerge his ego for the sake of what is best. Accessibility is not a matter of being unable to control situations, but a matter of being empathetic to the plight of others. Rigid leaders find it tougher to bring about change in others because they tend to be less trusted and more misunderstood.

The first step to leadership is the act of leading oneself before leading others. Being accessible is a matter of leading from the inside out. Apart from living a worthwhile life, there is a need for ambition, which requires taking reasonable steps before finding success. Accessibility gives leaders the chance to set their company apart from other businesses and to increase its growth. Organizations attract more customers and clients because accessibility opens doors for others to engage in the organization's activities. The fact is, one can only be successful if barriers are removed and an open environment exists for others to participate. However, without accessibility, it is difficult for effective communication to take place and businesses can suffer setbacks and visions remain dreams. Bear in mind that stakeholders do not invest their time and resources in expectation of excuses. Once a leader is unable to deliver what is expected of him in the interest of other stakeholders, decisions have to be made. Accessibility is a vital element for growth and progression to occur within an organization and it is everyone's concern. From experience, accessible leaders are well-known to be dependable, hardworking, and conscientious, always discharging their duties efficiently. In improving the level of accessibility within an organization, the three core aspects to be considered are effectiveness, efficiency, and equality. Effectiveness is the major parameter which enables leaders to accept the responsibility of defining success in developing a reliable system to a business. Efficiency is a channel to avoid waste, including waste of equipment, supplies, ideas, and energy.

THE ACT OF COMPETENCY

"I have no idols. I admire work, dedication, and competence.

"Ayrton Senna"

Peggy Noonan, an American author, said:" sincerity and competence is a strong combination". In leadership, politics and other aspects of life, competency is what it takes to produce effective results which could stand the test of time, value, and reality. The truth about the quote above is that leadership without competency is equal to zero. Factually speaking, competency is the ability to get things done effectively. However, competency is an organizational parameter which ensures that information is correctly processed and complies with relevant rules, procedures, and regulatory requirements. A competent leader understands the need to be accurate in terms of reviewing of his work and that of others to minimize error and works within the limits of his authority, seeking guidance when unsure. Leaders keep themselves up-to-date on current internal and external procedures and regulations while completing all aspects of allocated tasks. Competency needs to be assessed at various stages for projects to be successful. Competencies are divided into three main groups, i.e. core competencies, leadership competencies, and professional competencies.

Core competencies focus on learning, on-the-job experience, understanding terminologies, concepts, principles, and issues related to a particular field. The importance of this competency is its ability to enable team members to develop a good sense of responsibility. It's acquiring basic knowledge and skill by acquiring resources toward becoming effective. However, core competencies provide the foundation for growth in any field, such as good communication skills and expressing oneself effectively both orally and in writing. Good communication also supports plans and activities in a manner that upholds strategies for stakeholder engagement. Actively listening to others leads to making effective decisions. Effective negotiation skills such as getting reduced prices for raw materials purchased in large quantities and getting the best terms and conditions to settle differences with stakeholders within an organization. By using a win-win approach, we can maintain relationships which are the major reasons for an organization to embrace core competencies. Team building is another important competency because it involves organizing available resources to accomplish tasks with maximum efficiency within an expected period.

Professional competencies are the skills and knowledge required to adopt and operate systems and processes in an advanced manner within an organization. It's necessary for organizations to understand the requirements for each set of professional competencies regarding various leadership and executive positions. It involves the planning and implementation of strategies in the expectation of attaining a particular direction.

The practical side of team building is about using appropriate interpersonal skills to steer team members toward meeting organizational goals. This is achieved through gathering and analyzing customer feedback to assist in decision-making and improvement parameters. However, creative problem-solving techniques are also core competencies required when identifying causes of operational setbacks and collecting relevant information for possible solutions. This involves the use of brainstorming techniques to create a variety of choices for an organization to move forward. Core competencies are basic needs for managing client relationships in a flexible and reasonable manner.

Leadership competencies are the skills needed to drive an organization to the cutting edge of new technologies. These include a leader's ability to make stakeholders trust and support their vision and mission. This stage involves creating a vision and setting goals and making them realistic for others to embrace. Competency at this stage is about gaining the commitment of others by influencing them via objectives and buy-in on the process. It facilitates the ability to develop high-performance teams by establishing a spirit of cooperation for achieving goals that reflect effectiveness.

According to Richard Eleftherios Boyatzis, the American organizational theorist and Professor of

Organizational Behaviour, competency is defined as: "A capacity that exists in a person leading to behavior that meets job demands within the parameters of an organizational environment, and that in turn brings about desired results." In his work, various parameters are used such as efficiency orientation, concern about impact, proactivity, self-confidence, oral presentation skills, conceptualization, and others that are vital in embracing competency to achieve desired outcomes. The fact is that leaders need to be concerned with developing competencies that will enable them to be more effective in facing challenges and handling more responsibilities. It is wise for leaders to embrace the use of social intelligence in understanding and responding to social situations and dynamics. This provides the ability to operate effectively in a variety of social situations. Social intelligence as a whole is developed from gathered experiences while relating to people and learning from the successes and failures in social terms. Prudence is another factor to consider when talking about competency because a prudent leader listens to others and seeks their opinions regarding issues. In leading others, managers need to bear in mind the importance of building, maintaining, and sustaining highly successful and motivated teams who are consistently interested in achieving business goals.

When leading an organization, leaders need to know how to manage time effectively, communicate effectively, manage change, manage internal politics, and influence others in solving problems and making decisions. It's the responsibility of a good leader to know when and how to maintain relationships in and out of an organization to align its vision and strategy to produce excellent results. It takes the right competency to encourage others to improve their skills and have better levels of understanding in keeping the business moving forward. Competency enables one to remain focused and committed to a particular course of action by understanding the position of others and presenting arguments, facts, and figures in a way that is persuasive.

Competency is what it takes to develop, manage, and execute relevant strategies to make plans realistic, which creates value for the business. Competency also identifies the strengths and weaknesses of products and services in light of changing customer tastes and needs. In terms of making suggestions to increase competitive advantages within the industry, the need for competency can't be underestimated. A deep understanding of competency facilitates good decision-making because it enables leaders to make reliable decisions, taking into account the facts and feelings of others. Making use of past experience can be used as a guide in making decisions and analyzing available information for strategic purposes. Competency enables leaders to defend their decisions with reasonable explanations and also ensures that the right resources are available ahead of implementation.

The term competency is about driving results via genuine efforts, which refers to meeting objectives on time and balancing cost and quality. This is easily measured as it is entirely performance-based. The fact is that competency needs a strategic perspective, which enables leaders to have a clearer view of their organization's future. Competency is what is needed to remain accurate and relevant. This might be a broad definition, but without it, attaining growth might be difficult to an organization, because competency is required for planning and controlling; it enables fulfillment by establishing priorities, actions, relevance and reasonable constraints in a logical sequence.

A young man drove his car to the serving center, which would take more than three hours. A young sales executive approached him and said she had a surprise for him, it caught his attention. The young lady took him to the showroom and opened the door of one of the latest models, gave him the key and helped him put the roof down and gave him a pair of sunglasses, at which point he thought, "Why not paint the town red for the next two hours?" The young lady said, "Oh, that's nice" and off the young man went. While driving the car, he discovered some features which were missing in his own car, but he had never seen the need to get a different model. He drove home just to show off the car to his family and neighbors. They all loved it and initially thought it to be his. His children thought the car should be used to drive them to school, but the young man wasn't sure he should change cars or not. After an hour, he returned to the service center, where the saleslady was waiting for him at the pickup point. "Didn't you just love the car?" she asked. "Of course," he replied. "My family thought it was mine." The lady then asked the man, "Do you know why they thought that?" The man didn't know why. "Because it commands respect," she answered. The man then saw why he needed to change his car and asked what the new car cost, even when he had no plans to change his car. The fact is, if the saleslady always sold cars in such a manner, her career would be highly successful since she had such a clever technique of persuading customers to buy even when they originally had no plan to do so.

To sum it up, competency can never be achieved by magic, guessing, or just dreaming. It requires the reality of doing what needs to be done. It's the best way of meeting expectations to give the desired value and not by giving reasonable excuses. Competency requires having the determination for improvement, learning from the experts and at the right sources such as seminars, workshops, and webinars, investing in yourself by reading books and practicing to become better.

THE ACT OF CONTENTMENT

"Wealth gained by dishonesty will be diminished, but he who gathers by labor will increase."

Proverbs 13:11

Long ago in one of the smallest towns in West Africa, where land is a valuable treasure, a middle age man forcefully exchanged his land for that of his elder brother after his death. It took a serious conflict in which his cousin had to give up the moment one of his late father's friends testified at the king's palace that his father had handed over the land to brother before his sudden death. The fact was the man committed the act because the land had nutritious soil and his own land could hardly grow crops. After a number of years, a foreigner slighted the same land as the best location to relocate their business in which they need to lease the land from the rightful owner. Rather than his cousin leasing or selling the land, he decided to convert the monetary value of the land which he abandoned to shares which enabled the cousin to become a shareholder and later a director because he left the village to educate himself in the city. After realizing his mistake, he went to his cousin demanding for his land, the same issue was taken before the same king whom made a decision based on the testimony of the false witness whom he paid. The king imprisoned the false witness and banned the man from the village, which made him forfeit his land which was his major source of income and became poor due to lack of contentment.

Contentment is a vital aspect of leadership, a platform towards a feeling of greatness. However, it needs to be seen as a major parameter in developing ourselves and training the younger generation because this is the only way an issue such as corruption, poverty, and conflicts can be brought to an end. It takes discipline to distance oneself from immoral acts such as cheating and manipulating others for personal gain. It also facilitates the habit of being honest in one's relationship with others and oneself, it enables one to go for what he can afford and remain satisfied with the outcome. Contentment is not a matter of settling for less when more could be done to attain peak achievement but instead seeking improvement when the right resources are in place. It is paramount for those who desire greatness to be content with what they have at any particular point in time and remain consistent in working toward attaining greater goals in any endeavor because the key is doing well and doing it consistently. As Oprah Winfrey once said: "Be thankful for what you have; you'll end up having more. If you concentrate on what you don't have, you will never,

ever have enough." This quote points out why the lack of contentment makes a man live another man's life when he should be paying attention to his own.

One dictionary defines contentment as, "The state of being mentally or emotionally satisfied with things as they are." In reality, humans are rarely content with what they've gotten at any particular point in time. According to Buddha, "Health is the greatest gift, contentment the greatest wealth, faithfulness the best relationship." I wholeheartedly agree with this quote, because the desire to live a life based on integrity is the major reason one needs to be content with whatever he has. In general, contentment is simply a state of happiness and satisfaction. Contentment is a state of mind that you can achieve without becoming a monk. The fact is, contentment needs to be seen as a way of life before one's life can be worthwhile and be seen as a model for others.

Literally, contentment can be defined as the state of being mentally or emotionally satisfied with one's current lot in life. From experience, regardless of how rich or wealthy many are, they would always want more, like Oliver Twist, neglecting the fact many are to have a day meal, yet they have no compassion for their fellow men. Apostle Paul from the Bible wrote in the book **of Hebrews 13:5, "Let your conduct be without covetousness; be content with such things as you have."** Taking it from the perspective of integrity, acting from a state of covetousness reflects greed and selfishness. It's so easy for covetous leaders to suddenly find themselves in despair because covetousness soils one's personality and tarnishes one's chance of stepping forward in a career. From experience, I know that selfish people can be violent because they never give consideration to their fellow human beings when it comes to sharing benefits or returns, which later destroys them. They never understand the current situation or emotional state of others by living and acting nonchalantly. The Bible says in the book of **Proverbs 21:13, "Whoever shuts his ears to the cry of the poor will also cry out and not be answered."** Our life becomes meaningful and our world becomes a better place when we believe in the act of living and sharing with others in a contented manner.

However, in living a content life, we need to be disciplined and truthful in all we do, even when others are taking alternative routes which might seem to be right but could later backfire. King Solomon, the wisest and richest man who ever lived, said in the book of **Ecclesiastes 5:10, "Whoever loves money never has money enough; whoever loves wealth is never satisfied with his income."** In essence, HAVING the wrong desire for things which are not necessary is the main cause for many individuals quick downfall in life. In business, for example, the lion's share by one party is often the main cause while many growing businesses collapsed unexpectedly, in most cases makes one's life meaningless and could end up destroying him. I would like to take inspiration from the Bible in the book of 1Timothy 6. 6 – 9:

THE ACT OF CONTENTMENT

> *"6 But godliness with contentment is great gain. 7 For we brought nothing into the world, and we can take nothing out of it. 8 But if we have food and clothing, we will be content with that. 9 People who want to get rich fall into temptation and a trap and into many foolish and harmful desires that plunge men into ruin and destruction, 10 For the love of money is a root of all kinds of evil."*

Wise men never get motivated by money and the desire to be more creative is worth than the desire for money. For the sake of better understanding, let's take a critical view of the above passage verse by verse.

6) But godliness with contentment is great gain.

Understanding and living a contented life keeps one free from trouble because no matter what the state or situation might be, it would be easy to avoid misbehaving. The opposite of contentment is greed, which destroys one's capacity to enjoy what one has, or good intentions. The father of the political bulldozer never knew his misbehavior later destroyed his son's ambition at a time that would be too late for him to make corrections. I am sure he wouldn't have been the only one involved in such an undisciplined act, but for the fact that others got away with it didn't spare his own son from facing the music of what he had done before his son got floored easily at the debate. I am sure if he had predicted such incident, he would have boycotted it.

Many people eager to gain riches or wealth in a dubious manner wander from the reality of a nemesis catching up with them when they least expect it, mostly when making fatal decisions. I do marvel when top politicians and business personnel are held accountable by law for greedy behaviors while in a position of trust, influence, and power. The benefit of contentment goes beyond financial reward. It becomes easy to persuade others to embrace an idea without an element of fear or doubt because one's story of patience, endurance, and contentment would serve as a minor to others. It enables one to find joy at an old age, which reflects fulfilment, but a covetous desire creates more problems, mostly when corrections can no longer be made, it gives the mind unrest which leads to a shorter lifespan in some cases. However, when talking of great gain, I see a situation that could yield a great advantage, like a genie granting wishes in your life. The gain in practicing godliness and being content is huge and wonderful, but it requires being truthful to oneself and one's faith. Many had lost focus and insight of their calling due to lack of contentment in terms of what they should be, where they wanted to be and which part to follow. Many had switched from their right part due the outcome of someone else's in any field not understanding the fact that each man has gotten his appointed time.

7) *For we brought nothing into the world, and we can take nothing out of it.*

This passage reflects the whole reality of the human life span. Either rich or poor, tall or short, master or slave, the whole truth is we are sojourners in this world and shall leave the same way we came. To ground my fact, **1 Peter 2:11, "Beloved, I urge you as sojourners and exiles to abstain from the passions of the flesh, which wage war against your soul.** "Apostle Paul's advice in this passage alight the word *passion of the flesh* as things that bring short term enjoyment and long term ruin. In reality, *which wage war against your soul*, indicates situations that cause regrets, disgrace, and reproach. The desire to attain any position or acquire anything through a covetous manner makes one's life worthless and meaningless. It's good for one to work hard for a just cause and build one's life. I do say countless times, living for the purpose of another man is the best way to waste one's life. To live the best of one's life it's essential to have an insight of what you want to be, where you want to be and how to get there, rather than living each day the way it comes and slugging and fighting for what is not necessary. I do say countless times, it's unreasonable for a man to die for what would not be of any use to him while in his grave. It's not a must to have everything but its reasonable and wise to cherish and share with others the little you have. Taking insight from the book **of Ecclesiastes 1: 2, "Vanity upon vanities, saith the Preacher, vanity of vanities; all is vanity."** And coming to verse 14: **"I have seen all the things that are done under the sun; all of them are meaningless, a chasing after the wind."** I pity the greedy one's because they lack the required understanding to live and remain content in which makes them learn the hard way, they live big to end up nowhere. **Proverbs 13:11,"Dishonest money dwindles away, but whoever gathers money little by little makes it grow."**

A contented man would never end up regretting his life no matter what the case might be because they would cherish and enjoy whatever they have and they love to share with others. I would like to reference the CELESTIAL CHURCH OF CHRIST hymn book 291: **Let's harken to the message of our creator, to earn his glorious reward, the world and its riches varnish but the truth, but the word of our creator endures forever**. However, the above extract could justify in **Isaiah 40:8, "The grass withers and the flowers fall, but the word of our God endures forever."**

8) But if we have food and clothing, we will be content with that.

Traditional and immediate needs of humans are food, shelter, and clothing. The reality is other needs are immaterial because one can do without them. In most cases, our backgrounds, belief, opportunities, and environment determines what we get from life and where we stand in it. The most important thing is that one should be thankful and contented with what one has. Contentment creates stability, and as the old saying goes, "The grass is always greener on the other side." If we never find contentment where we are, we will continually be driven to new places in search of more and end up wasting more resources. Many people go into debt to buy the newest model car instead of investing in a small scale business to enlarge their holdings. Many buy over-priced phones because they boast updated features. Contented people have no need to change course or direction for the sake of change, which creates a more stable lifestyle. Contented people are focused on going the extra mile with what they have; they only go for things they can afford and not for the sake of fashion or impressing others.

9) *People who want to get rich fall into temptation and a trap and into many foolish desires that plunge men into ruin and destruction.*

Studying this passage, it is clear that covetousness pushes one to fall into trouble, which determines one fate in life if proper care is not taken. The fact is avoiding covetousness keeps one's head above water and gives peace, which money can't buy. One thing I have noticed is that money becomes useless during trouble. Doing the right thing at the right time and as expected is the best way out of trouble. As the Bible says in **1 Samuel 15:22 "To obey is better than sacrifice, and to heed is better than the fat of rams."** However, it is not wrong to possess money and material riches, but it is wrong to acquire wealth in a dodgy manner and later run into unexpected troubles. In today's business and political world, people do commit atrocities and deceive the public for their own interest of becoming rich, but are always afraid of accountability before the law and hardly live a life of peace. Many people with a huge tendency of living a bright future and going beyond expectation have lost it all by betraying their values which they are well known for because of money. They compromised their good intention for money by being dishonest, disloyal, and untruthful to their calling and later tarnish their legacy for the sake of money. I am yet to see money redeeming a tarnished image where all things are being equal.

In mid-summer of 1984, the collapse of a huge pharmaceutical company became the headline of most prints and digital media. There was a huge consistent protest of the shareholders on the grounds that the situation was created by the executives because no one ever predicted the situation from the previous annual report. However, during an interview, the chief executive officer blamed the situation on the change of government policy on international trade and their losses were a result of huge foreign tax payments and poor diplomatic relationships with countries they traded with. The angry shareholders never accepted that for an answer because the insurance company was reluctant to indemnify the shareholders, however some of the shareholders, who were also employees of the company, could not support the chief executive officer after he had addressed the issue in a press conference, calmly he was playing the double standard game. The situation led to a public investigation and just in the middle of the investigation, the team leader of the investigation, who was appointed on the belief to be a man of integrity, made a sudden request for a change of team members based on the grounds of incompetency and lack of effectiveness of the investigating team assigned to carry out the task. Cutting a long story short, the investigation was conducted and concluded with an "all is well" report in which he was awarded by various organizations and the insurance company was forced to indemnify the shareholders.

Nine years later, after sleeping dogs had being considered lying, a new headline captured the media nationwide regarding the acts of the team leader who was, at this point, selling his coach hiring business and fleeing with his mistress. The wife of the team leader revealed how she advised him not to be dishonest but he chose to do things his own way. The wife didn't stop at this point, but tendered the genuine documents regarding the investigation of the collapsed pharmaceutical company and alighted to the fact that she was sure that monetary reward for the cover-up was used in starting his coach hiring business. However, this led to a public outcry and a police investigation. From the police findings, it was clear the collapse of the pharmaceutical company was as a result of the bank loan obtained in the name of the company but was paid into separate accounts which were kept secret from the shareholders and some executives were buying products with the company name and not remitting funds to the company account, while many suppliers were owed quitea huge sum of money. However, it was discovered that the chief executive and some senior officials registered another company that imported low-cost products from other countries and were selling these with the company's brand on it. These transactions earned huge money and affected the company in a negative manner. Further investigation revealed the reason the team leader was recommended by another investigating team, which was actually an auditing firm that was owned by the brother-in-law of the chief executive. It turned out that they both helped the company executives in "cooking the books" and manipulating financial reports.

The police discovered that the team leader operated a joint account with a certain woman who happened to be the former personal assistant of the chief executive of the pharmaceutical company. The very same woman later became a shareholder at the team leaders company in which the team leader's wife wasn't aware of because the team leader was smart in his own way by having two sets of documents regarding the investigation. Upon interrogation, the mistress, whose account was used in paying the team leader for his dishonest behavior, revealed how she was brought in into the game with a plan to seduce the team leader and to friend him to keep things on track. The whole turmoil began when the chief executive was down with a serious stroke and was demanding his personal assistant to allow him to see his two children as he had lost his only son in a motor accident. The team leader was believed to be their father and she has refused to grant his

THE ACT OF CONTENTMENT

request because of his failing health and did not want her children to be fatherless. She then persuaded the team leader to escape with her and the children. Unfortunately, unknown to the team leader, the chief executive had written the team leader's wife and included this woman's picture. However, after the confirmation of a DNA test it was clear that the chief executive was the biological father of the children.

To sum it up, the team leader was later jailed for his illegal participation and became a nobody in the society while the chief executive died. The personal assistant was given a suspended sentence for the purpose of caring for the children. The team leader's love of money made it easy for him to buddy up to the chief executive and dance to his tune. His love for money made him compromise his total self, became dishonest with his wife who filed for a divorce and made him lose a huge percentage of his wealth. He had the entire awards withdrawn at the interest of a public protest and ended up regretting his actions. Only if he had known and understood the reality of Proverbs 17:1**: "Better a dry crust with peace and quiet than a house full of feasting with strife**." He would have escaped the trap he fell into if he had stuck to doing the right thing and not being smart. Those who are content with what they have are always humble, happy, and blessed.

10) For the love of money is the root of all evil. Some people, eager for money, have wandered from the faith and found themselves with many sorrows.

Coming to the point, money is good, but the love for it is the root of all evil. For the sake of clarification, the book of **Ecclesiastes 10:19, "A feast is made for laughter, and wine maketh merry; but money answereth all things."** In most cases, craving wealth leads to evil, apostasy, ruin, and destruction. Many go after wrong desires in life for the sake of competing with others around them. They are well known for inferiority complexes, i.e. ensuring they belong to a certain class of people which pushes them toward the wrong track and commit wrongs to enrich themselves. For the purpose of clarity once more, being wealthy or rich through creative means is never bad, because the Bible made it clear in **the Proverbs 20:13: "Love not sleep, lest thou come to poverty; open thine eyes and thou shalt be satisfied with bread."** In reality, *open thine eyes* means to be wise and creative in terms of being productive, while thou shalt be satisfied with bread means being blessed abundantly. Poverty is never desirable, yet gathering riches in an unjust manner leads to a fall. This fact is proven in **Jeremiah 17:11:"Like a partridge that hatches eggs it did not lay, there are those who gain riches by unjust means. When their lives are half gone, their riches will desert them, and in the end, they will prove to be fools."** Many have lost their life's passion, their calling, and things that could have given them joy due to the love of money. **Vanity upon vanity, all is vanity according to King Solomon in Ecclesiastes 1:2.**

Reading the story of the Covetous Neighbour by Katherine Neville Fleeson, there was a poor and lonely man who had but a few melon seeds and grains of corn which he planted. Tenderly did he care for them, as the garden furnished his only means of a living. And it came to pass that the melons and corn grew luxuriantly, and the apes and the monkeys from the neighbouring wilderness, upon seeing them, came daily to eat of them, and as they talked of the owner of the garden, wondered just what manner of man he might be that he permitted them unmolested to eat of his melons. But the poor man through his sufferings had much merit, and charitably shared his abundant fruit with them.

And one day, the man lay down in the garden and feigned death. As the monkeys and apes drew near, seeing him so still, his scarf lying about his head, with one accord they cried, "He is already dead! Lo, these many days have we eaten of his fruit, therefore it is but just that we should bury him in as choice a place as we can find."

Lifting the man, they carried him until they came to a place where two ways met, when one of the monkeys said, "Let us take him to the cave of silver." Another said, "No, the cave of gold would be better."

"Go to the cave of gold," commanded the head monkey. There they carried him and laid him to rest.

Finding himself thus alone, the man arose,

gathered all the gold he could carry and returned to his old home, and with the gold, he built a beautiful house.

"How did you, who are but a gardener, gain all this gold?" asked a neighbor, and freely the man told all that had befallen him.

"If you did it, I too, can do it," said the neighbor, and forthwith he hastened home, made a garden, and waited for the monkeys to feast on it. All came to pass as the neighbor hoped; when the melons were ripe great numbers of monkeys and apes came to the garden and feasted. And one day, they found the owner lying as one dead in the garden. Prompted by gratitude, the monkeys made ready to bury him, and while carrying him to the place of burial, they came to the place in the way where the two roads met. Here they disputed as to whether they should place the man in the cave of silver or the cave of gold. Meanwhile, the man was thinking thus, "I'll gather gold all day. When I have more than I can carry in my arms, I'll draw some behind me in a basket I can readily make from bamboo," and when the head monkey said, "Put him in the cave of silver," he unguardedly cried out, "No, put me in the cave of gold." Frightened, the monkeys dropped the man and fled, whilst he, scratched and bleeding, crept painfully home.

This fact is, lack of contentment is the platform for living a shameful and regretful life. A lot could be said about contentment, as the Bible says, in 1Timothy 6. 6: "*Godliness, i.e.* having a great reverence for your faith in a consistent manner in combination with contentment will eventually produce great gain, benefits or rewards." Lessons from the story reflect covetousness as a parameter for making one lose opportunities and keep one stagnant. Covetousness had forced many to learn the hard way and many have lost their reputations and fortunes as a result of it. Contentment reflects our ability to adapt wherever we find ourselves with a reasonable amount of patience. Note that every patience needs to be for a purpose, reasonable, and worthwhile, else the situation might lead to stagnancy. When practicing contentment, one needs to appreciate whatever he has gotten and never run through another man's watch by trying to live in another's world. One needs to bring his desires down to the level of his possessions in a realistic and positive manner, and remain hopeful in terms of attaining success and being fulfilled. Having watched countless of people caught in the act of crime over the media, I realize that most of them ventured into crime because they wanted to be successful and command respect like that politician, celebrity, or superstar mostly when comparing themselves to others based on their age, education, and other factors that command respect within the society. The fact is, a huge portion of today's society had misunderstood the meaning of success in real context, however, success is not achieving something through manipulation or harming the next person in order to enthroned. According to Dr. Prabin *Shresth; Success does not lie in "Results" but in "Efforts", "Being" the best is not so important, "Doing" the best is all that matters.* In reality, this quote is meaningful and simple, *Suc-*

cess does not lie in "Results": many do enrich themselves through dishonesty and never have a peaceful night like the chief auditor whose shameful efforts was later opened up to the public unexpectedly. I do remember that he paid someone to help write his final dissertation after being awarded a better grade by the first marker, the internal and external verifier agreed to invite the student to defend some statement which was believed not to be a reflection of the student understands. After some hours of questioning, he admitted he paid someone to write up the final dissertation and was penalized because the final dissertation wasn't his effort and a reflection of his understanding regarding what the writer wrote. In a nutshell, if success lies in efforts and not in the result, then success lies in facing the reality and risk of taking reasonable steps, making commitments, and improving outcomes at various stages and make positive impacts. If success lies in results alone, it would be easy to get things done by deceit, exploiting others, and manipulating situations and do away with such acts. However, for success to be valuable, the ends would have to justify the means. The main reason why people with great vision or desire fail is they only after results and not willing to understand the rough processes in involved in getting great things done. However, ignoring accurate process in any endeavour is the foundation for failure.

The second line of Dr. Prabin *Shresth quote is* another powerful statement which makes a lot of sense.*"Being" the best is not so important, "Doing" the best is all that matters.* Only if Benjamin

THE ACT OF CONTENTMENT

Sinclair commonly known as "Ben" Johnson wouldn't have involved himself in doping which made him lose his Olympic and World Championships titles. He finished up as the best in those competitions but was disqualified for not doing things the best way. Also, the world of athletics would never forget the grace to grass story of Lance Armstrong, who ended his athletic career due to doping allegations, the painful part of the story was that he was later also stripped of all of his achievements after 1998, including his seven Tour de France titles. He took himself to be the best before regarded as an icon in the cycling world simply because he never understood being the best is not so important but doing things in the best way is what matters; he loses all he had achieved in his career time. Bear in mind, results are good but not the best indicator of success and those after results in an aggressive manner don't go far most times due to their insufficient ability to learn the best ways of getting things done. Being and doing the best is always as a result of learning, according to Tony Buzan, the English author and educational consultant said and I quote, *Learning how to learn is life's most important skill. However, learning never ends.*

Understanding the act of contentment is often the result of having resolved a difficulty or achieved a goal, making one have a sense of satisfaction. The fact is, contentment creates the platform for stating reasons for our actions and not giving excuses. Contented leaders find it easier to lead by example because the situation reflects their personality like a mirror, which makes them connect and win with others. Note, for a fact, that when we are content this shouldn't make us aim or settle for less. In a place where more could be achieved, more effort should be made to live our lives to the fullest. Bear in mind, discontentment in a positive and reasonable manner enhances the zeal for one to be the best in any endeavor, the zeal for peak achievements in a man acts as a catalyst for change because fashion gets outdated regularly. A lot can be said about contentment, but the fact is it is self-developed, which requires the ability to let things of value go for the interest of peace. Contentment is a product of one's endurance in waiting. It is the price for maintaining peace because it involves the ability to consider others before any personal interest or ambition. Waiting patiently is never a crime because it brings comfort. Patience in life can make us reach out beyond expectations and can enable us to avoid making hasty decisions that we could later regret. Proverbs 10:22: **"The blessing of the Lord brings wealth, without painful toil for it."** Above all contentment is the soul of integrity.

I would like to finish up contentment with story of two young friends who were labourers in one of the countries in East Africa. While at work on a particular day, an old woman passing by greeted them and warned them never to fight or depart each other for happy days ahead of them. As the days pass by, so likewise the months and the years they both kept on with their friendship until a particular marabout came to introduce the advantages of a wealthy kingdom to them. After a while of looking confused, he promised to revisit them a few days after, as to give them time to be able to make their up minds. After the day's job, both friends decided to give the situation a thought. One held on to the old woman's word while the other began to doubt her of the time involved, he never knew where she was from and never saw her again. In short, out of sentiments he changed his mind. A few days after, the marabout revisited them while one was asleep, the other decided to leave a note saying "*Alternative routes are not bad, life is short.*" and followed the marabout who had now been accompanied by two other men. When the sleeping friend awakes, he was shocked and was so worried that his friend could not wait for the right time, suddenly the old woman appeared and congratulated him for his patience and gave him an ancient wooden cup and told him to go and to wait till the cup is called on. So the man went to the third village from his previous state. When the friend who went after alternative got to the wealthy village, the first rule was read which was no one brings in anything into the village, as a matter of fact, he'd have go nude and hinge his clothes on a nearby tree before going in. After many years of trading and accumulating so much wealth, he decided to return home to settle with a family of his own, as foreigners were not allowed to marry indigenes. While he got to the entrance of the village, about exit, the second rule was recited to his hearing that none of the village wealth goes out of the village. At this point, he became confused of what action to take. After a few minutes of meditating, he decided to go back. Then the third rule was recited, all items brought to the entrance shall be forfeited by their owner and if he chooses to go back he would have to start all over. What a mess? The man asked himself, but nobody ever told me this, the site men then replied if he had bothered to ask anyone? As a matter of fact, he decided to leave the wealth village; he was made to leave the same way he arrived and went for his old clothes on the same tree where he hanged them. While he was tracing his old in friends with tears, the same marabout appeared and began to laugh, cackling can you see all that glitters is not gold? Meaning that not everything that looks precious or true turns out to be. You deceived me, he shouted at the marabout, no, I only did my job, likewise the old woman whom advised you and your friend not to part each other. The wealth village is a forbidden land, where no one trades and makes profit and it's meant for impatient people like you. The marabout knew he was tracing his old friend and he was told how to find him and disappeared while others were laughing and cackling. After a few days, he found his old friend at the exact location being told by the marabout. He wept bitterly while he expressed his regrets of going for the alternative route. After some days, he asked his friend how he was blessed, then the patient friend began by how the old lady later revisited him after he departed and gave him an ancient cup and showed him the next direction to take. On getting to the third village, the king of the village was seriously ill and the only remedy was the king to drink palm wine from an ancient cup. The announcement was made and a day was scheduled for whosoever had the required ancient cup for the king would enriched by the king with money and huge portion of land. Cutting the long story short, this was how the patient friend became rich. The impatient friend wept all over and regretted his action. The bottom line is, contentment goes along with patience and alternative routes are not always the best. To justify my point, Proverbs 14:12: **"There is a way which seems right to a man, but in the end it leads to death".** However, the word *death* in this passage reflects a state of regrets and disappointments. Contentment is having the right desire and not covetousness, I do remember the first line of the third verse of the CELESTIAL CHURCH OF CHRIST Hymn book 694, **in vain is it for a man to desire earthly treasures that would vanish**.....The reality is wise people are never motivated by money for sudden wealth but doing what they are passionate about in which brings about happiness.

THE ACT OF EQUALITY

"I have a dream that one day on the red hills of Georgia, the sons of former slaves and the sons of former slave owners will be able to sit together at the table of brotherhood."

Martin Luther King, Jr.

Generally speaking, many do interchange equity for equality. Equity is about fairness in ensuring that everyone is assisted according to the required needs of various individuals. While equality of opportunity is about treating people without any form of bias i.e. the same way. In life, certain situations might make some people unequal with their peers but it's the major responsibility of an effective leader to ensure that those who fall behind are not left behind by giving the extra support to reflect equality. It's about creating a situation that encourages and values diversity and promotes moral respect. The best of any leader is always reflected when discretion is applied on the grounds of age, disability, gender, race, religion, political beliefs, sexual orientation, or marital status. Equality is about treating organizational stakeholders on the same terms, which makes leaders' actions justifiable. Without equality, no leader can claim integrity, which makes it necessary for leaders to understand deeply how to lead and relate to others without any form of partiality. In an organization or a state where equality is well respected and practiced, responsibilities are distributed equally among all team members or stakeholders in a reasonable manner. It's a state where no individual is regarded as superior to others and everyone is allowed to contribute his quota and take part in sharing benefits. Every contribution made by a stakeholder in a state of equality is always cherished by others, no matter how small and is also seen as a positive influence in meeting set goals to a large extent. However, it becomes easier to table, develop, and promote positive ideas for the future of an organization.

It enables leaders to strengthen their ability to stand up for their vision both individually and collectively, i.e. working and winning with a passionate, genuine team. Relating to others equally increases their capacity to influence people through effective communication and powerful feedback. Over the years, the issue of promoting equality has been a legal requirement that ensures everyone is treated fairly, given equal access to opportunities, and not subject anyone to unlawful discrimination. Diversity takes this a step further, promoting inclusiveness by ensuring everyone is valued as a unique individual and respecting differences.

Many mistake equality for diversity, but they are two different things. Equality is about treating people in the same manner while diversity is about ensuring that all stakeholders have the opportunity to maximize their potential and enhance their self-development and contribution within an organization. Equal opportunity in the workplace is not only good practice, it also makes good sense in enhancing a good reputation for an organization. An equal opportunity policy will help all those who work within an organization to develop their full potential, utilizing their talents and resources and maximizing efficiency for peak performance, while increasing the level of effectiveness and maintaining low turnover. Treating people equally enables us to examine ourselves in a genuine way because it's about putting ourselves in other people's shoes. Equality is a better way to build mutual trust within any organization because it's about seeing others the same way we see ourselves and also prepares us for better opportunities. There is no way a leader could be regarded with integrity without having a sense of equality. Equality needs to be promoted within an organization by treating all stakeholders fairly, creating an inclusive culture for all and not neglecting others for any reason and ensuring equal access to learning and development.

Fairness is another aspect to be considered when talking about equality. It takes a man to be fair before he is able to treat and see other people equally. According to H. Jackson Brown Jr., "Live so that when your children think of fairness, caring, and integrity, they think of you." Only those that are fair in their undertakings are considered worthy of leading others. Fairness is an application of empathy in the way we relate to others in order to make the world a better place to be. Fairness needs to be seen as a professional skill that must be developed and exercised because it's the only way to drive things forward. In law, fairness is a principle allowing for the use of discretion while handing out justice. The term fairness simply means being impartial, unbiased, and unprejudiced in every situation. Fairness is characterized by equality, respect, justice, and humility in all situations.

In leadership, fairness is a high virtue, because it's the major platform from which effective leaders give others a voice and treat them with dignity in a consistent manner. Fairness is one of the hardest qualities to define, but it has a lot to do with avoiding bias, treating people equally and allowing people to have equal chances to do things or express themselves. Fairness also enables leaders to base their decisions on accurate and complete information, which increases their worth as respected leaders. Fairness does not always mean the same thing to everyone, as this could cause leaders finding themselves in challenging and controversial situations when trying to please everyone in order to avoid conflict. Fairness is relating to stakeholders and giving them the opportunity to voice their concerns regarding a particular situation. Good leaders respond with clarity and also carefully evaluate their interests before making strategic decisions.

The hidden fact about the positive impact of fairness within an organization is that fair managers and leaders earn more respect than those who believe in the use of power and force to make others do things. Fairness makes it easier to handle complex situations and carries others along. Leaders who embrace fairness are more likely to achieve unexpected goals because their team members want to give their all to get things done, even with insufficient resources, whereas leaders who believe in the use of power generally experience confrontations due to their proclivity to punish people for little or no mistakes. In most cases, others are always wary of giving their best because of their leaders' dominating attitudes and often see them as stopping blocks to promotions.

Fairness is not pretending to be nice but behaving in a way to earn the trust of others in a cordial way. Fairness is about giving others what they deserve at the right time and in the right manner. Fairness is a factor that needs to be considered when communicating policies and guidelines to others regarding the future of an organization and also the major parameters considered before arriving at such decisions. Effective leaders never blame or punish people for what they did not do, and they appropriately sanction those who violate moral obligations or laws.

Fairness is about being open to feedback because this is when leaders are seen as good listeners. They keep the communication lines open with team members by asking questions and reflecting on the answers. Some leaders believe in the use of their power or office to get things done, but fairness is about getting things done through credibility and the use of building respectful relationships to influence others for positive change. It's about being flexible, honest, and impartial. Fairness is all about being open and responsive to the needs of others, which requires leaders to adjust their behavior and interests to best match the situation. In organizational leadership, fairness is setting clear and reasonable criteria for performance reviews, promotions, raises, or bonuses, disciplinary action and qualification for various benefits. It's also about truth telling, promise keeping, and respecting individuals as oneself. However, fairness is the major quality that facilitates greatness and equality in leadership. Leaders who don't like conflict bring greatness to their team by explaining collaboration and its importance. Fairness lies in accountability to the team's success. From a natural understanding, fairness is about caring about the interests of other people and being sensitive to their needs rather than being self-centred. Fairness within an organization lies in overcoming self-doubt to ignite each team's success. To be fair means to be justified in one's relationship with others, and the Bible says in Proverbs 21:15: **It is a joy for the just to do justice, but destruction will come to the workers of iniquity."** The fact is, human life takes on a godly character and fairness is lovely and kind, it's all we desire and deserve in all we do to ourselves and others. The beauty of fairness is lasting joy, which money can't buy. Equity and fairness need to be part of any leader's character to help them attain greatness; however, without these two qualities, hardly anyone associates with such a leader due to fear. Fairness is not imposing your personal opinion on others regardless of what the result might be. Fairness also means impartiality in the sense of not taking sides on an issue where there is a dispute. It also entails presenting all sides of an argument fairly to draw a balance.

THE ACT OF LOYALTY

"Confidentiality is a virtue of the loyal, as loyalty is the virtue of faithfulness."

Edwin Louis Cole

Taking insight from the Bible in the book of Proverbs 3:3, **"Never let go of loyalty and faithfulness. Tie them around your neck; write them on your heart."** Loyalty is an essential quality of our daily life. It's about having a strong assurance regarding someone else, be it work, business, family, or friendship, because loyalty is about the major characteristics of anyone regardless of their background, gender, and profession. Loyalty is the state of being faithful to commitments, obligations, causes, and people. Being loyal to oneself and your calling is the major platform toward fulfilling one's purpose in life because it channels one in the right direction with discipline and the right mind set. The fact about being loyal or not is that no matter how dodgy one might be, reality can't be overshadowed because one must be tested at various points and times in life. For a man to be identified with significant loyalty, he must pass the test of value, time, and reality. The test of life reflects who a man is and the cause he stands for, regardless of what the situation might be. Loyalty is about holding onto and practicing whatever is believed and accepted to be right. Bear in mind the test of confirming loyalty is never easy. Being loyal is a matter of being ready to sacrifice what it takes for the sake of what is right. From life experience, many have found themselves in a state of being disloyal simply because of personal gains or fear of the unknown. Taking insight from the life of Apostle Paul in the Bible, he said in the Book of Philippians **1:21: "For to me to live is Christ, and to die is gain."** One fact about Paul is that he was courageous to speak the truth without fear, even while in prison. However, he wrote fourteen books of the New Testament which were based on real life. Paul was a man who was loyal to his calling which gave him the boldness to write in the book of 2 Timothy 4:7**, "I have fought a good fight, I have finished my course, I have kept the faith."** He made this statement with all confidence because he was sure of his loyalty toward what he stood for. His sincerity to his calling with all humility and respect made his life and words worthwhile, which made him a man of integrity. Taking inspiration from one of the songs by Lynda Randle, "God on the Mountain", in the first verse she mentions, "Life is easy when you're up on the mountain, and you've got peace of mind like you've never known." What a state of comfort. But a loyal man can only be known and sure of himself until the challenges of the deep and dark valley occur, where he is being faced with the option of either bearing the pains of standing and fighting a worthwhile course or compromising for whatever reason.

Loyalty is not just a vital element in any relationship, but also an essential quality because it facilitates the trust required to build legacies and recognition on a daily basis. The fact is that loyalty is displayed through love, devotion, dedication, and commitment to the well-being of another, either at work, business, in family, friendship, or a relationship. It takes loyalty for a man to genuinely apologize for a mistake and ensure it doesn't occur again. Lack of loyalty is one of the major causes of failure in every walk of life. It requires one to be self-disciplined and content to be loyal, people fight and struggle unnecessarily for what wouldn't last as long as expected. Being loyal is a matter of being determined, focused and committed toward doing what is right at the expected time and at the right place. Such was the case in the story of the sower in the Bible, Matthew 13:8, **"Still other seed fell on good soil, where it produced a crop a hundred, sixty or thirty times what was sown."** Those seeds that were able to produce never fell on the path for the birds to eat up, which is a reflection of no impact. Some fell on rocky places, but could not stand the test of time due to the insufficiency of soil nutrients. They recorded little growth about the seeds but stood the test of the sun. The plant didn't grow because of the limited extent the root could go in terms of struggling for its survival. Coming to the seventh verse, some seeds fell among thorns, which grew up and choked the plants. This is the result of those who venture into various endeavors without having a clear understanding of what the future looks like. They do things out of confusion and cannot go far, having their expectations cut off without foreseeing it or becoming stagnant at one point or the other. The good part of the story is about those seeds that endured, staying in the hand of the sower, and getting to experience the result of being loyal to their calling. While in the hand of the sower, they couldn't be comfortable due the controversies of coming off his hand before arriving at the good soil which had all requirements to produce up to expectations. Those seeds reflect those who stay focused, determined and gave what it takes to be fulfilled, which is commonly known as endurance. One major fact is that loyal people never lose their faith, even when others have lost their faith in them. They believe in making things right when and where they go wrong, they make necessary adjustments.

For any relationship to last longer, partners always need to trust and understand each other and the only to earn the trust of the next party is by being loyal and not by imposing based on status. There is also a need to be willing to sacrifice whatever it takes to move things forwards. However, in leadership, loyalty needs to be shown to all stakeholders in an equal manner, because a crack in the wall could lead to the collapse of the whole building if proper care is not taken.

Loyalty is to be considered mostly on the side of the customer because a complaint could lead an organization's reputation into being compromised and loyalty is a unique reflection of what a man or an organization stands for. Loyalty is a vital quality in leadership because it enables one to take responsibility in a sincere manner and let go of things which are of value to others in a courageous manner.

The act of loyalty brings out the qualities of leadership. One doesn't need to a leader or a super model to be loyal but needs to be loyal to be an effective leader. It enables a leader to recognize the value in other people, so as to continually relate and invest in them wisely. Loyalty enables one to live with an above average character and uses their influence for the betterment of others and for the success of their organization. Loyalty makes it easy for others to see one as a role model, because of the act and will to support and serve others without expecting anything in return. Loyal people believe in continuous learning from all that occurs around them, this is also the secret of improvement and not by magic. Loyal people are not afraid of making the right decisions and never dodge facing challenges. They are accessible, approachable, and accountable to others. They never isolate themselves from the right people regardless of the amount of responsibility or power they attain. Loyal people stay in line with their vision, they consider any form of diversion a defeat and they are good at thinking.

THE ACT OF RELIABILITY

The most reliable way to forecast the future is to try to understand the present.

John Naisbitt

A promising young lady who happened to be a sales executive once showed up at an interview for the position of a marketing manager in another company. After answering a series of questions at the panel, she then asked to give details of her company's marketing strategy. Rather than being diplomatic and keep it confidential, she went ahead and detailed it before the panel. She was appreciated and was promised to be contacted. While on her way home, she got a phone call regarding the unsuccessful state of her application, after she asked the necessary question which as 'why'. She was made to understand that position is a sensitive one and it's meant for those who are mature and can maintain a huge level of confidentiality. Furthermore, she was also informed that employing her would be more of a threat than an opportunity because she has a huge tendency of revealing the company's strategy to a competitor within the industry in the nearest future. The bottom line of the story is, only if the young lady had been diplomatic, she wouldn't have been considered unreliable. Reliability reflects the value we live and stand for, come what may. It needs to be considered as a way of life as previous records would always be considered when looking into the future. As humans, we need to understand the West African proverb our deeds are traceable and all current acts later become historic. Only if the father of the bulldozer had acted in a reliable way while in office, it would have been easy for his son to get elected into public office in his lifetime but he wasn't and took it public as an opportunity to enrich himself.

From the way we live our lives and relate with others from different backgrounds and perspective, it's paramount we maintain a better level of responsibility, reliability, and being realistic in all we do. However, it requires one to be realistic before they can be counted on in any situation. In any research work or questionnaire, it's important that facts and data are collected from a reliable source that reflects honesty, to then be used in making strategic decisions. Reliability is about doing what is profitable such as wise usage of time and reasonable investment. The bible made clear in **Proverbs 14:23: "All hard work brings a profit, but mere talk leads only to poverty"**. In a real sense of life, it requires taking reasonable steps in any endeavor for anyone to prosper and not just knowing what needs to be done. When talking about reliability, its goes a long way in having a specific level of expectations regarding a subject matter in terms of exchange of value. For example, reliable cars are expected to save time and money on repairs, reliable mail is expected to get delivered on time and reliable investments are expected to deliver expected returns. Furthermore, reliable airlines are expected to take off on time and land safely. So likewise, reliable restaurants are expected to have quality food and service.

Reliability in itself is of huge importance in psychology, leadership, and other aspects of life. At various times, we do depend on people getting things done following a particular set of standards. It is crucial that anyone who is depended on is also reliable to produce the expected results, rather than making excuses or something that can be questioned for false representation of certain subject matter. In a nutshell, reliability can also be defined as the relative absence of errors in measurement. From experience, many do take the words responsible and reliable as meaning the same thing. To clear the air, being responsible simply means that you are liable to be called to account for or be morally accountable for one's actions. While being reliable reflects someone of consistently good character, they are also thought of as being dependable and trustworthy. Being reliable is a vital part of leadership regardless of the type of situation that presents itself. In reality, it takes one to be responsible for being reliable. It takes the proper understanding of responsibility to show up to work on time, be prepared for meetings and be trusted to work without constant supervision. While being reliable requires the individual to keep track of one's actions to achieve whatever is being expected of him or her and not making excuses. Another word for reliability is dependability, which means that a leader or anyone can be relied on to perform their duties in a proper manner and with integrity. For anyone to reflect reliability, the individual must be able to accomplish any agreed task by finding ways around possible obstacles.

According to Larry R. Kirchenbauer, the leadership guru, "In some ways, being reliable transcends many of the other essential qualities of leadership because people need to depend upon you under all circumstances. You might say that your constituents, whether employees, customers or vendors, demand your Reliability — because they also rely on you to be Loyal, to pursue Excellence, to have a positive Attitude, to be Disciplined, to Educate yourself and your team ...", the qualities of leadership we covered earlier in this series. Without the act of reliability, it becomes hard to be trusted, given the benefit of the doubt, foster loyalty or instills confidence in others. The unbeatable fact is reliable people receive greater opportunities which could transform their life for the better. Once tested and considered reliable, other people can count on them for larger responsibilities with better rewards. Reliable people live with confidence, integrity, and clear consciences because they keep their promises and obligations. Not only can other people count on them, but a reliable person can count on themselves.

Being a reliable person is a huge sacrifice, it enables one to be identified with integrity and to be taken for real. It's about keeping one's promises, i.e. being a person of your word and not saying one thing now and doing something else later on while justifying your changes with excuses. It requires a huge sense of reliability to fulfil one's promise. A reliable person would never overpromise no matter how high the pressure might be. A reliable man would only promise what is realistic and achievable, having the knowledge of what is available and what is expected. Reliability requires one to understand how best to manage expectations, especially among various groups with a conflict of interest. Being reliable is also about communicating effectively regarding any task or project that involves others. Doing things without effective communication with the right people at the right time is a pathway to failure. Bear in mind, poor communication prevents effective execution. However, reliability is not just a matter of doing a task for the sake of doing it, but doing it well to stand the test of value, time, and reality. Being consistent with what is right is a huge part of reliability and integrity as a whole. People who lack consistency fail to gain the trust of others. The reliable man develops consistency by setting goals for himself that stretch and challenge him but are do-able day after day. Being reliable involves planning effectively before taking action or making decisions because when assigned a responsibility and then failing to make the right predictions, it becomes easy to underestimate or see one as unreliable. Reliability is about upholding one's values, ethics, morals, purpose, and so on. Reliability of an individual should not be contingent on circumstances or try to be like someone else. Reliable people never give up when the unexpected situation occurs because they would have prepared ahead for the possibility of such a situation which, in turn, reflects their value in the long-run.

Some believe leaders are born and become natural leaders. Others believe leadership can be taught and anyone can become a leader. Some do become self-made leaders; state leadership is situational and when intentional can be very powerful. The point is regardless of the platform of leadership without the act of reliability, the situation would end up being meaningless. Reliability is one of the foundations of teamwork and cooperation. It allows people to work together, with the person doing what he or she does best, knowing that friends, family, or co-workers are taking care of their respective tasks. Being reliable is an extremely important quality to have, especially in areas such as customer service, sales, and marketing. It's paramount to prove to clients that one's reliability by being honest is in one's words and actions. This honesty is one of the most fundamental aspects of customer retention and having your present customers refer new friends and customers. However, the more one proves themselves to be unreliable, the more opportunities and investments could be lost. Being reliable and not pretending makes our relationships with others last longer.

Reliability in leadership is about standing the test of value, time, and the reality of a leader in terms of having the unique attributes such as superb character traits, knowledge, skill, abilities, and behaviors. However, the mentioned attributes are aimed at making leadership more effective in any situation by enabling leaders to learn from the key experiences of great and successful leaders. Having read a lot of books written by great leaders from various backgrounds across the globe, I discovered they are all responsible in terms of having the zeal and ability to take action at the right time and never blame anyone for their mistakes. They just try harder the next time having made the necessary adjustments. Great leaders are realistic in terms of representing things in a way that is accurate and true to life and not assuming or making decisions based on sentiments. The third common attribute in great leaders is that they are reliable, which makes it easy for others to count on. When considering reliability in a deep context, I would like to consider three levels of reliability; i.e. ability to lead one's self, ability to lead people and the ability to lead an organization.

The ability to lead one's self-goes a long way in demonstrating honesty, trustworthiness, and integrity where ever one finds himself. It's about doing away with selfishness, pride, and arrogance as these are the major platforms for failure. The ability to lead one's self-enhances the opportunity to understand one's reasonable vision before sharing it with others with the expected level of intelligence for the betterment of all. It's expected of a reliable person to have a good sense of judgment to avoid conflict or confusion when transacting or relating with others. It also deals with self- discipline, and humility because one without discipline and humility could do anything for the sake of money regardless of the outcome. The ability to lead one's self-makes them a role model for others to follow, boost one's level of confidence, and provide an atmosphere of optimism that will influence a positive attitude on others.

One major fact we need to understand is that no one can lead others without having the ability to lead him or herself. How can one who is not diligent and intelligent in his output direct others? Surely the outcome would be unexpected. In reality, leading others requires having respect and caring for others before connecting with them with an effective communication style, mostly in the aspect of listening which makes it easier for others to believe they are being carried along. It entails demonstrating trust in whatever one does as a leader to inspire and motivate others to take action that could enhance a positive change or transformation to their lives. The ability to lead others includes the ability to monitor and assess the capabilities and performance of others and produce a reasonable feedback for the purpose of improvement. Every effective leader would always know and understand the fact that people need to be nurtured and taught to perform at a reasonable standard via training, coaching, mentoring, and other developmental measures to update and improve the skills before delegating tasks and expectations. However, leaders need to know how best to hold people accountable in a fair manner rather just punishing for every single mistake they made.

Within an organization, it requires a reliable leader with a clear vision to motivate others towards driving growth. In a nutshell, no one can achieve their dream without being reliable and taking the reasonable steps required towards it. Reliability is important to increase a company's profits and improve brand reputation. One of the aspects of reliability is that it touches many groups within an organization. Both in the short- or long-run, the sole aim of reliability is improvement and improvement can only be attained by learning and listening to others. No leader, in whatever situation, can reflect integrity without being reliable because it means following through with what needs to be accomplished to attain success or excellence in any endeavor. It is a reflection of acting on the words spoken and not saying it just like a slogan. In terms of being an effective leader, there's a huge need to understand the organization's vision and believe in it in terms of it being achievable via effective planning and the ability to demonstrate a commitment to making every organizational vision a reality. Every organizational leader must have the ability and insight to make decisions to enhance a positive situation at any time. Organizational leadership can be productive by getting the right people on board and promoting teamwork at all levels of an organization. For peak results to be achieved, leaders need to encourage participation and bounds consensus for action among team members. To place the icing on the cake, it's paramount for leaders to understand that leadership is about carrying others along via influencing and persuading them positively i.e. with a zero party system to action towards delivering a peak performance in a coordinated approach and just imposing and dominating people to achieve expected results at all cost. According to Prabin Shrestha, "Success lies not in the result but in the effort. Being the best is not at all important, doing the best is all that matters. As a leader, doing the best needs to be paramount than the result because when capitalizing on what to be achieved and not how to achieve it, there a huge tendency of an error occurring in which might cost more to adjust or repair. The case is similar to an operation manager concerned about producing thousands of drinks without caring either the machine is in proper shape to produce the required quantity if a breakdown occurs within the process of production such a manager would be considered to be up unreasonable and incompetent. As a coach, I do clear the air that both leadership and management do share, the ability and the obligation of planning and coordination of organizational activities, providing the required motivation for things to move forward within an organization and evaluate organizational performance to maintain a better position within the marketplace and edge out competitors. In leadership, reliability is a matter of managers and leaders having the ability to manage commitments both at work and private life. It's also about respecting the time and walking the talks. For leaders and managers to consider as reliable, they need to be knowledgeable, self-motivated, creative, ethical and humble. In today's business and political world, passing new laws or formulating new policies is not all that the solution to existing issues but implementing those laws and policies in the interest of all stakeholders as expected.

To sum it up, reliability is a reflection of maturity in terms of speaking the truth, regardless of the situation. Be a good listener and talking less is another trace of maturity because learning is the cornerstone of improvement and no one learns without first listening to others and learning is the major for turning falling or disappointing situations for the better. It requires maturity to admit when you wrong and not take offense in all situations. Reliable people are supportive and know when to act before being told, they seek peace and pursue it mostly when in a position of leadership. Maturity as a whole, is the application of wisdom of all aspects of life and not competing with others. It's learning for the sake of improvement and not outsmarting others.

THE ACT OF TRANSPARENCY

"Truth never damages a cause that is just."

Mahatma Gandhi

Mahatma Gandhi will always remain an icon in world history due to his views of religious pluralism in promoting the peace and unity of India as a nation. Transparency is more about standing up for causes that are blameless, honest, just, and true. To demystify the fact, transparency is making complex situations clear in creating a positive reflection for the future. In the political world, when politicians talk about making government more transparent, i.e. tabling their actions regarding everything that is happening before voters who happen to be the major stakeholders in deciding their fate in taking over public office or not. In reality, most politicians later formulate laws to prevent the public from having access to information on how the taxpayers' money is utilized. It's easy for anyone to attain the position of a ruler in any situation and such would be considered to be a leader on the grounds of sentiment, but not everyone that rules can lead, because effective leadership is all about understanding its principles and not just knowing it. In has become a common and acceptable practise in today's business, religious and political would to present inaccurate information and making it look real all in the name of confidentially and cover up their shady activities, the pure and hard truth is, where nothing to hide, transparency is possible. The need for transparency will always be on the rise because it's a major quality expected in any leader and once lacking, the hope and future of team members remain in the dark due to high levels of doubt and uncertainty. Transparency is about sharing accurate and relevant information with expected stakeholders at the right time. It's also about encouraging questions and answering them in a clear manner. Transparent leaders are well respected for their passionate attitude in seeing others become more effective and not passing judgment on others for their mistakes. Such leaders are interested in seeing the action, decisions, and relationships being legally and morally sound in order to pass the test of time and value to yield significance within an organization.

To be transparent as a leader has gotten many different meanings, but the common one is the ability to be consistently behaving in a way that is predictable and flexible. It's a way of boosting one's worth as a leader in terms of being candid, honest, and genuinely expressing one's thoughts or opinions. It's also about consistently keeping commitments, handling one's own defeat, learning from them and not blaming others. Valuing the feedback of others and getting others on board to gain their support is also vital to being a good leader. To build a transparent organization and leadership style, leaders, and managers need to be approachable and treat others at every level within the organization with humility and respect. This is also the cornerstone of attaining effective performance. Another point is that leaders and other senior figures need to be in accord, i.e. everyone is on the same page regarding the organizational view of the external environment in terms of defining corporate goals and implementing plans for an organization. However, leaders need to come on board with reasonable ideas in establishing transparency to improve the efficiency of corporate operations and bolster employee satisfaction, ensuring that the reputation of the organization is in good standing to deliver other benefits to both internal and external stakeholders.

One of the best protections against organizational or government corruption is transparency, and in today's digital age, one of the easiest ways for the government to be open and accountable is through posting public documents on the Internet in order to strengthen the level of trust and accountability. From all indicators, online transparency has successfully been the best approach in fighting government corruption and wasteful spending practices, which has become the standard way of governing in most first-world countries.

Transparency in leadership is more efficient in problem-solving as a result of laying all the cards on the table from the outset. There is easier team-building through the open acknowledgment of group's strengths and weaknesses, and authentic interpersonal relationship growth between members of the organization. Transparency facilitates greater trust and respect for organizational leaders as a result of presenting them in a more human light. Without transparency, there is nothing like integrity, because it's all that is required for leaders to lead and transform organizations to achieve great results because over time they have built solid relationships based on their character. Transparent leaders are reliable, predictable, and committed to serving and supporting their teams. As such, they are trusted and easy to follow, which allows them to achieve their goals when transforming an organization.

Specifically, transparency is a major parameter which strengthens institutional credibility and public trust because it reflects openness. Transparency enables external stakeholders to understand anorganization's operational strategies to grant their expectations, provided that leaders explain the procedures, structures, processes, and assessments in simple terms to ensure the smooth running of the organization. In practical terms, integrity leaders ensure that their actions are seen as trustworthy and creating a sense of certainty rather than uncertainty. They exhibit openness with respect to information, finances, and various operational transactions and business dealings. When examined by others, their actions lead to trustful relationships.

To be transparent anorganization must be open to its stakeholders about its activities and performance, providing basic information to them on what it is doing and how well it is doing it through financial statements, annual reports, and performance evaluations. This is the basic information needed by stakeholders to monitor an organization's activities and to hold it accountable for its actions, goals, and objectives. However, to be transparent, an organization must do more than disclose standardized information by providing stakeholders with the information they require to make informed choices and decisions.

Transparency is a matter of communicating information based on facts, not assumptions. Acknowledging what is needed to be known in order to learn and develop from others is important. It's a matter of sharing progress, challenges, risks, issues, and blockers among team members. As a leader, transparency is a matter of having the ability to lead others without fear or confusion, because it entails being intelligent and having a stable character. Transparent leaders are well-known for their ability to let go for the sake of peace. However, lack of trust reduces transparency and effective communication; it also reduces innovation and causes lack of agility and responsiveness to changing conditions. Trust in leadership can increase performance easily because of the level of compassion increases among team members. However, where trust dwells team members feel respected, recognized and appreciated for their contribution. As a leader, you need to understand the vitality of compassion in gaining the trust and commitment of team members, because it's a reflection of trust and without it, one is completely off the track.

In corporate governance as a whole, transparency is a sensitive area which deals with the handling of information, disclosure, clarity, and accuracy of all actions in relationship to resources and earnings. To increment transparency, corporations need to infuse greater disclosure, clarity, and accuracy into their communications with stakeholders. Transparency creates assurances for stakeholders in terms of their investments because it deals with areas such as monitoring the activities of entrusted directors. To hit it home, listening is critical in reflecting transparency and also in building trust, because without listening, leaders would find it difficult to understand their team and other stakeholders need for both professional and personal guidance. The fact is without having the appropriate understanding complex problems can never be solved, and goals can never be attained no matter how skillful a leader is.

No one can claim to be transparent and be able to maintain a stable and healthy relationship in any situation without being honest because it reflects reality instead of fantasy and it's also a platform to avoid harmful breaches of trust. Being transparent involves the accurate application of knowledge in balancing stakes to avoid conflicts while being honest entails knowing yourself and your intentions, making your actions match your words in most situations and being sincere about your reactions in a consistent manner. In today's business world, transparency spreads far beyond reporting for the sake of it. It entails reporting the right information to the right stakeholder in the right format at the right time with the right intention. Some of the importance's of transparency are its ability to solve faster, help in building effective team easier and enhance growth in an authentic manner. When leaders are transparent, people can be much more objective in evaluating the pros and cons about their leader.

THE ACT OF DISTINCTION

"Every person has a longing to be significant; to make a contribution; to be a part of something noble and purposeful."

John C. Maxwell

Human life is a process which needs to be action - and goal-directed due to the free will of making choices at various points in life, regardless of the situation being faced. As humans, we need to come across situations in which we need to determine whether we give up or give the situation whatever it takes to step up. Either we fight or fly from challenges, either we settle for less or we strive for the best we can be. The only thing that gives our lives real meaning is our ability to pursue our purposes at the right time, but the only power or free will available to humans is known as choice. Being purposeful always occurs as a result of being focused and determined in a consistent manner towards fulfilling our purpose in an expected manner, and not as a result of a do or die affair. Apart from being focused and determined, there is a huge need to identify, know, and clearly understand our purpose and the cause we stand for as humans irrespective of where we found ourselves. I would like to suggest you read "The Mysteries of Excellence" by Emmanuel Goshen to understand more about this point. Another point to consider is the act of setting and embarking on the right priorities by spending more time on the important stuff, drawing a balance between one's needs and wants in a realistic measure. It's paramount to determine and keep one's goals in a clear state of mind to avoid confusion. In being purposeful, there is a need to be well organized and updated when making plans for the future so to avoid being stuck at an unknown junction. As generally known, one tree can never make a forest, so likewise it would always serve great importance to realize that one can't do everything, which makes it paramount to seek the support of others. Enthusiasm is another aspect to be considered in living purposefully because it's an avenue in remaining energetic and interested in one's unique purpose in avoiding failure.

However, the purpose is a conscious, intentionally chosen goal, which needs to be pursued for the desired outcome. People of purpose live and relate to others respectfully and intelligently in which distinguishes them. They also lead effectively with a passion and not with a divine and rule style. They aim at being purposeful to encourage those around them and help them live a meaningful life. Bear in mind, one who is not purposeful in his ways would eventually be wasteful. It's reasonable to understand strategic processes before making moves in any situation. One of the things to be considered in living and being purposeful is the act of being resourceful in all relationships and dealings because the fact is no one can pour tea into a cup from an empty teapot. A man can only give what he has and not what he doesn't. It's not wise to be a pleaser to all with nothing in the bank for a rainy day. The point is, in any situation, it's wise for one to know and understand potential benefits before making ties or moves.

I mention in many seminars and coaching classes we should never grab an opportunity without understanding the terms and conditions in full. No reasonable organization would ever draft terms and conditions which would either be a strategic trap for them or that would create a platform for any of its customers to take advantage of them. They are always mindful of playing technical games with the legal obligations of their business, else the long arm of the law would force them to pay penalties than they do expect. This is the major reason why one needs to carefully consider the conditions before making decisions under every circumstance. The fact is, being authentic, reasonable, and realistic in every situation are the major parameters in living a purposeful life, i.e. making a positive impact for oneself and others. In living a purposeful life, one needs to acknowledge his source of income and expenses before making commitments to avoid unnecessary struggle in any situation. Maximizing the value of one's income by spending and investing wisely is important because saving and not investing money in a growing business doesn't enhance its real value in the long run. It's wise to invest in one's personal development because it's a way of updating one's knowledge concerning the changes occurring in today's world. Investing income into a new business is a good way of increasing opportunities and the possibilities of maintaining satisfactory financial status. As an individual, the need to take responsibility can never be underestimated, anyone aiming to live a purposeful life should never think to escape from his problems mostly in the aspect of understanding the negativity the problem could create if not attended to. Reality cannot be bought or sold; it can only be faced head-on and the outcome is either one wins or loses. As humans, we need to be independent in our thinking, which enables us to challenge our assumptions and strengthen our determination to rise above limitations in a sensible manner. Never allow fear to keep you from moving forward because your ability to handle and face challenges reflects your level of growth and it also creates a platform to deal with obstacles and make them steppingstones to better opportunities. If fear is allowed to delay any organizational process, the impact on time and other resources wasted would always be regrettable. However, it is paramount to attack one's fears in the early stages in a positive manner. No matter what happens while in the right and standing for the right cause, never take, talk, or allow defeat, always remain hopeful of a better tomorrow. Never fear to fail, but always seek improvement and not perfection or trying to be like someone else. According to Marie Curie, "Nothing in life is to be feared, it is only to be understood. Now is the time to understand more, so that we may fear less." And, Napoleon Hill, the American author once said, "Fears are nothing more than a state of mind." The reason for fear is never reasonable because no one will pay to invest in fear and people who fear never start a race and those who never start never win the race.

The fact is, attaining excellence is realistic based on how one thinks of parameters such as hope, faith, and victory, which reflects one light to others around. The primary key for us to be fulfilled in life is for our mindset being guided by having the right thoughts while going in the right direction and taking the required steps. Always be aware of who you are and what you want to be, and don't allow anyone to impose a false belief on you or reshape your future. Never believe in impossibilities regarding attaining your goals, because no goal is beyond one's reach with the power of focus and self-discipline. Purposeful living involves living your life with a purpose of fulfillment for yourself and for those with whom you are in relationships with your spouse, children, friends, co-workers, neighbor's and yourself. In living a purposeful life, it's paramount to make today count and not give excuses as to why ideas don't work but learn the required and different steps which could change the situation around. In some case, the idea might be right but need the right people to communicate it with. In being purposeful, never give up your hopes and aspirations for the sake of anything, because it's no meaning to work halfway only or another man to get the reward, so aspirations are worth keeping alive and giving it whatever it takes to achieve one desired. Another fact is, starting late doesn't mean one can't overtake those ahead, provided one is serious and remains consistent in the right direction. I recommend reading the seven laws of productivity for a deeper understanding.

The act of leading purposefully is the platform to convince others about the need for change where necessary. However, in leading purposefully, there needs to be a better understanding of a specific mission in order to make the change process meaningful. There are three major components to leading others purposefully: 1) Engagement 2) Empowerment and 3) Encouragement. In analyzing those three parameters one by one, I would like to consider more of their positive impact.

When speaking of engagement in leadership, it's a result of understanding the required commitment in moving an organization forward. It's about living and leading the right way to give one better meaning. However, engagement is having the required energy to change for the better of all stakeholders. It's a matter of bringing the right people along in achieving the overall mission of an organization. It's a matter of understanding overall strategy and the implementation processes in making the organizational vision a reality. In engaging others, it's paramount for leaders to ensure that their team members' perception of any mission is a positive one, or else the quality of the expected picture might suffer in the long run. It's the job of an effective leader to educate an entire organization, from the top down. Educating team members increases the level of being clear and confident about an agreed-upon direction. In engaging others in any situation or project, it's essential to make them know and understand the importance of what is to take place and the impact of their expected contributions, which is required to make plans a reality. However, a leader who is unable convey the big picture before engaging others may create confusion, and the act of engaging others needs to an authentic platform toward attaining excellence in an effective manner.

In engaging others in any initiative, it's vital for any leader to understand the concepts in ensuring that those involved in such initiatives are happy to be carried along, provided they have a clear understanding of what benefit are to be derived, both materially and intellectually. However, they need to be satisfied at the end of the project. Another vital point to be considered when engaging others is that an effective leader needs to bear in mind that he is in control with a sense of direction and responsibility about whatever outcome is attained, or else the issue is similar to trying to drive a car, but the steering is being controlled by someone sitting in the passenger seat. In reality, the driver, in this case, is a typical example of deactivated leadership, i.e. holding a position without a sense of control and direction, which is a leader without impact. Having a sense of control enables one to determine future performance in a visionary way, which is the cornerstone accomplishment. The fact is, effective performance is the key toward meeting the needs of stakeholders and not the act of giving excuses. No matter how intelligent a man might be, the moment he starts avoiding taking responsibility, he begins to distance himself from better opportunities, because excuses would always prevent one from attaining and fulfilling bigger goals in the future. Bear in mind, excuses are not friends, no matter how beautiful they are, and they can never enhance productivity in any sense. In my experience as a life coach, I have discovered that excuses indicate a lack of understanding in how to get things done as expected with sufficient resources. A serious determination can never be defeated under normal conditions. It's impossible for anyone to claim to be a person of integrity without being able to show what he has done or what he can do in terms of performance. Another aspect to be considered when engaging others is the creation of a platform for growth as a way of helping others develop their strengths. However, this can only be realized by being open to learning from their output in terms of identifying weakness and what the problem and its cause were in order to give the right support in improving performance, which is also another way of adding value to an initiative.

According to the well-recognized Canadian author, Robin S. Sharma, "Showing leadership doesn't mean every employee will run the organization; that would lead to chaos. Leadership could be reflected in one's relationship with others. If well-connected with those engaged, transformation becomes easier to achieve and a better level of overall improvement is attained.

Empowerment is based on the idea of giving team members the required skills, resources, authority, opportunity, and motivation to act and be fulfilled in specific settings. It also means holding them responsible and accountable for the outcomes of their actions. Empowerment is a platform for contributing competence and satisfaction to one's overall performance. It's a common practice of sharing relevant information, rewards, and power among team members to take the right initiatives and make decisions to solve problems and improve the service and performance of an organization. In reality, leadership isn't defined by the job title or opportunity to rule over others, which is a mistake many leaders do make. It's about developing one's perspective, skills, and personal style in leading others to get expected results. Empowerment is not forcing or imposing ideas on others, but influencing others in a visionary way to adopt a positive and possible mindset in going the extra mile for the betterment of an organization. Investors and top executives are well-known for telling directors and senior managers that they were hired for the purpose of achieving results, which will be justified by performance. Leaders who desire peak results need to develop and empower others to deliver expectations via effective communication and not thinking of getting things all alone, which makes a situation similar to the strong man who carries or pushes a full truck all alone as if his ability could be compared to getting a tow truck. Empowerment is never rocket science, it's a platform which helps leaders and organizations face key challenges by influencing others in attaining a new vision without the use of authority.

Empowerment sparks new ideas and concepts throughout an organization, including ways to reduce waste and increase productivity and efficiency. Additionally, empowerment improves relationships among managers, leaders, and employees, which correspondingly reduces complaints and grievances. In reality, an empowered workforce experiences an increase in terms of job satisfaction and also fosters better relationships with all stakeholders to produce a higher quality product or service, which enables an organization to enhance a better reputation in public sight. Another reason for empowerment within an organization is to develop and establish a win-win culture, which is always as result of looking ahead of execution to close the door against inconsistency. Empowerment is the soul of effective customer service; it enables team members and other stakeholders to understand the vision of an organization and to make their customers record an excellent experience, which is also a platform to attract and retain more customers. The unbeatable fact is that empowerment needs to be seen and taken as an internal branding system used in equipping oneself and others ahead of better opportunities because it's the cornerstone in reflecting what an organization stands for. The unbeatable truth about empowerment is that for anyone to be prosperous in any endeavor, his soul needs to be empowered in order to see challenges and obstacles as steps towards one's breakthrough and not as reasons to give up. Empowerment is the parameter which makes one's determinations meaningful because it fuels the determination and accurate performance anyone.

Encouragement is a powerful tool in motivating others because it increases the zeal to go the extra mile, it's a reflection of creativity and positivity of what an individual can achieve. Encouragement focuses on an effort expected to be carried out mostly when in an unpleasant situation and makes the necessary adjustments. It is a better platform to set up one's mindset for success and take action or make decisions on merits. When most people become frustrated in their life's career due to business or jobs and can no longer see light at the end of the tunnel, all they need to get encouragement is to study those whose lives were transformed by experiencing significant drama. However, words of encouragement bring life to the weak-hearted and restore people from states of hopelessness toward being hopeful. From a realistic point of view, encouragement is a platform to give others courage, to inspire them with the spirit of possibilities and hope to increase the level of confidence to pull down barriers and challenges while bringing out the best in them to achieve their goals. Encouragement enables one to overcome timidity or reluctance in any situation. It provides the required energy to accomplish objectives and also enable the act of living one's life with value.

Words of encouragement are the spark that gives us hope, mostly when in the dark aspects of our lives because it motivates us to take one small step after another until we see the light when in the middle of trials and challenges. One with courage is a majority and can go miles, according to the seven laws of productivity. Encouragement helps people change their perspective for the better, even after nursing negativity for a long time. When leading others and getting confused, it's paramount for an effective leader to encourage people to remain focused and keep emphasizing the bigger picture, which will enable them to make the right decisions in attaining their dreams.

The desire to live a worthwhile or purposeful life is the major reason why one needs to embrace encouragement as a way of life. The same desire is the major parameter which creates differences among leaders, mostly in their style of leadership and the results they attain. There are other numerous reasons to be purposeful and be distinguished in life, because according to Lord Alan Sugar, "What you see is what you get." In reality, whatever result a man realizes at the end of an expected period is directly proportional to the effort he made. Integrity is living a fulfilling life, which is achieving one's dream according to John Maxwell.

Another aspect to be considered when leading others with a purposeful vision is that it's unfair for any leader to see or regard anyone as being irrelevant. They need to be seen and taken as a responsibility to help make them relevant to what they do. To be recognized as a competent leader, it's essential to understand the negative impact of indecision in a situation where the stakes are high and learn how to drop what's not working or what is an unnecessary cost to an organization. They need to ensure that all parameters are relevant and reliable before being used to avoid conflicts.

It's paramount for leaders to reflect and share new ideas and understanding with others to enable them to be better than their previous selves and not just criticizing or judging them by their mistakes. In leading others for a purpose, it's vital to develop and prioritize winning moves to avoid stagnancy in any situation, which creates a good platform to be on guard against being edged out of business by competitors.

By and large, I do remember the hymn, when the roll is called up yonder? I will be there when, easier said than done, either we admit the fact or not living a life of honesty is the best legacy anyone could and pass to the next generation, yet never easy because it entails standing for what is right and not just what is good. Integrity can never be defective in the long run because being smart is just for a short-term gain and long-term loss. From my research, being honest is the only platform that could change our world for the better. However, the change needs, to begin with leadership in any situation and not shifting their responsibilities to their followers because for the world to be a better place everything hinges on leadership. However, leadership is an act of taking full responsibility, mostly in terms of positive change or transformation, because leaders can only give their followers what they have and not what they don't. Without beating around the bush, the major parameter in leadership is the ability to influence and make others a better version of themselves with skills and attitude. However, all great leaders keep working on themselves until they become effective, mostly in terms of making decisions and standing by them. Integrity is invisible in nature, yet it could be reflected in one's sincere undertakings and relationship with others. Matthew 5:37**: "But let your 'Yes' be 'Yes', and your 'No', 'No'. For whatever is more than these is from the evil one".** Bear in mind, for anyone to attract quality people, one needs to be a person of quality because leadership is the ability to attract someone to the gifts, skills, and opportunities. For one to be honest in any situation, one needs to learn to be strong but not impolite, learn to be kind but not weak, learn to be bold in saying that which is true but not a bully, learn to be humble and realistic but not timid, learn to be proud of your efforts and whatever you have but not arrogant, learn to develop humour without folly and learn to deal with realities and not sentiment.

TAKE THIS HOME

"Discipline is the bridge between goals and accomplishment."

Jim Rohn

To commerce the last lap of this book, no matter how rich, educated or fortunate a man might be, integrity is what matters. i.e. the positive impact created for others to minor. No matter how beautiful a goal might be, how strong a determination might be or talented a man might be, without the discipline to accomplish it, the task remains difficult. Discipline is the only platform that keeps the ability to be focused and committed on track toward accomplishment because without discipline all invested effort toward a certain task would be meaningless and wasteful. Taking insight from the quote stated by Jim Rohn, one of the greatest American motivational speakers that ever lived in history, his rags-to-riches story played a large impact on the lives of many toward becoming someone better than they used to be. Jim Rohn made it clear in many of his speeches that discipline makes one a person of influence for positive change because it becomes easy to persuade others. Self-discipline gives one the power to stick to one's decisions and follow them through without being inconsistent andis, therefore, one of the important requirements for achieving goals in attaining a specific direction. Self-discipline is about fulfilling promises made to oneself and to others. It's the best approach to overcome laziness and procrastination, which is the act of making one responsible.

To make it clear, leadership or any lifestyle without discipline is as good as meaningless, and according to Lou Holtz, without self-discipline, success is impossible, period. For anyone to live a life based on integrity, the need for self-discipline can't be ignored, because it's the only platform to keep one out of unnecessary competition, which has been the cause of many downfalls and places one on a path to success with the ability to be focused consistently.

Self-discipline enables one to remain committed to one's future and vision by avoiding diversions. Integrity commands respect, but only for those who are able to attain expected goals. Self-discipline facilitates the act of passing good judgment regarding situations and abilities within an organization. It requires a proper understanding of self-discipline before one can attain milestones in any endeavor. Achieving greatness is one of the major outcomes of self-discipline, but it requires the breaking down of one's vision into measurable goals, with timelines to make them reasonable and possible to attain. Having interviewed leaders within various sectors on the benefits of self-discipline, three qualities are attached to self-discipline, i.e. honesty, which is about being truthful and open in all undertakings, while objectivity is basing one's advice and decisions on a rigorous and genuine analysis of evidence. Another quality is impartiality, which is about acting solely according to the merits of any issue and treating stakeholders equally. Success or failures are both terminals, but the ability to stand and pass the test of reality and value makes one's life and leadership worthwhile. Self-discipline brings about self-respect and makes one's actions free from bias.

Integrity in leadership is about the adherence to moral and ethical principles, i.e. soundness of moral characters, such as the courage to tell the truth in a constructive manner, the willingness to make tough decisions for the betterment of an organization and its stakeholders. Leaders need the ability to remain transparent to what is working and what isn't for the purpose of clarity. Only those who understand the consequences of lack of discipline would consider a second thought before involving themselves in actions that would either ruin their career or restrict them from utilizing better opportunities which could improve their skills and make their lives worthwhile. I consider it painful and shaming when a medical doctor with over twenty years of practice was reported falsifying medical reports in exchange for money, which are considered legal and acceptable documents even in a court of law. The situation lead to a serious controversy, only for the cat to be let out of the bag by a nurse who was considered to have cheated in the deal, a person with such a reputation and integrity became a criminal. I am sure no practicing doctor would ever consider him a role model because the medical world depends so much on trust and integrity a breach of trust occurs, the situation becomes meaningless. In order to make your story worth telling and your record presentable, you need to consider embracing integrity right from the start, because accountability is always an issue everywhere. There is no need to compromise any values, provided you know what you are doing.

The Bible states it clearly in the book of Galatians 6:9, **"And let us not be weary in well-doing: for in due season we shall reap, if we faint not."** In reality, reaping would take place after a certain period, which is the major point to stay any good course without fear. If we faint, the importance for humans to endure any good cause needs to be maintained. For a leader to be respected and treated with dignity. Leaders need to believe in the ability of their team members, so likewise the cooperation of stakeholders can never be underestimated or taken for granted.

Integrity is about relating to others with a sense of humor and living an upright life and not being involved in dodgy events, just because many others are getting away with it. The fact is, integrity is an issue of showing one's difference among others. According to the Book of Proverbs 14:12, *"There is a way which seemeth right unto a man, but the end thereof are the ways of death".* Integrity is about living above selfishness and the desire for it in one's undertakings makes one understand the importance of life and the need to play games by accepted rules. It's also about fulfilling promises to oneself and to others by avoiding excuses, which is the best way to overcome laziness and procrastination. The world never celebrates those who have nothing to offer.

To summarize, nothing works out for the betterment of mankind without integrity. leaders needs to know and understand their inner values and act in accordance with fairness, also work alongside with other like-minded to go beyond personal limitations in terms of building a lasting tradition for the next generation. When reality is ignored or taken for granted, it becomes impossible to impact lives positively. Without integrity in terms of walking the walk, it would be hard to maintain satisfaction among stakeholders. Integrity needs to be seen as a value, which everyone needs to strive for in all areas of life to make it worthwhile. The purpose of maintaining integrity within an organization is to sustain a good reputation within the industry and keep ahead of competitors. This act can open many doors for organizational expansion.

Choosing to lead and relate with integrity is the best approach anyone can take. Bear in mind, people always love to lead others with integrity, because it's a vital ingredient in motivating the ability to perform and go the extra mile. Integrity is not a matter of withholding relevant information but creating a relevant platform for effective communication.

I do remember the story of the young and promising doctor who forged a medical document and swore in a court of law, claiming to be genuine, but came up with a second edition of the story in light of the nurse whom he cheated in the deal. I am sure he will never forget the ridiculous state he found himself in, and his family was ashamed of him. Another fact is that records reflect one's past more than words and can be used in predicting one's future, as in the case of Mr. Bulldozer. The bottom line of the story is that one's character is either stable or unstable and will always be attached to one's name in an indirect manner. King Solomon wrote in the Book of Proverbs 22: 1, **"A good name is rather to be chosen than great riches and loving favor rather than silver and gold."** In reality, riches come and go, but one's name in relationship to one's impact is created either positively or otherwise, is always remembered.

In terms of safety, it has been proven beyond a reasonable doubt that leaders with a strong foundation of integrity make it safe for their team members to perform at their peak. Safety reflects the fact that the future is secure, all things being equal because a reasonable leader would take the responsibility upon himself in ensuring others become a better version of themselves. Such leaders believe in empowering others by giving them the required freedom to act respectfully and appropriately. However, when considering references, leaders need to understand and perform up to expectations in order to set the standard for team members.

Beyond all reasonable doubt, it's never easy to live a life totally based on integrity, but the ability to stick to what is accepted to be the truth and getting things done in a correct manner yields unlimited blessings. The Bible says in the Book of Mark 10:25: **"It is easier for a camel to go through the eye of a needle than for a rich man to enter into the kingdom of heaven."** In reality, it's hard for us as humans to practice truth on a full scale. It takes a lot of discipline and courage to live a meritorious life. Reading that passage of the Bible, the task is so huge that man is left in a discouraged mood. Integrity is often equated with courage. It entails the ability to speak and stand up for what is right and for the interest of others before one's own interest. Integrity is a great perspective because it points out the view of becoming responsible and great in life, and it's a commonly held belief about how things should be done for the betterment of mankind. Bear in mind that people identified with integrity are regarded with dignity, because no matter how rich or educated one might be, integrity is the cornerstone of living a worthwhile life.

According to one of the greatest musical legends that lived in history, Bob Marley said: "The greatness of a man is not in how much wealth he acquires, but in his integrity and his ability to affect those around him positively." In reality, the ability to embrace integrity as a platform to positively affect those you lead makes you a great leader, regardless of the position you hold within your organization. However, integrity is the greatest virtue in leadership, because it makes leaders effective.

My last advice before ending here and getting ready for the next book is that it's good to have one's dreams fulfilled, but it only becomes worthwhile if it is attained in a proper way. Settling for less or choosing to live comfortably in a vacuum is never the best way of life, so therefore working and living by example is the only authentic way forward. Integrity is the art of being purposeful, starting from the point of being responsible and accountable for one's actions in a reasonable and sincere manner. Being accessible in one's relationships with others in all aspects by not making issues complicated before anything can be achieved, cannot be emphasized enough. Competency is a major requirement in attaining success in any endeavor as it's the key to getting this done effectively. However, contentment is about being satisfied with whatever one has along with the hope of attaining more in the right way. Equality is about seeing, relating, and treating all stakeholders in a fair manner. Transparency is the platform toward being open to new ideas for the purpose of progress within an organization. When talking about the act of loyalty, it's about staying authentic to one's calling and determination toward making a positive, lasting impact in the lives of others and being purposeful for the sake of mankind. Integrity is not all about knowing every theory but about doing the best to achieve the required at any point, in a consistent manner. Being honest in all endeavors is the best approach to reflect a life of integrity and place behind a lasting legacy.

www.ingramcontent.com/pod-product-compliance
Lightning Source LLC
Chambersburg PA
CBHW070623300426
44113CB00010B/1641